GLOBAL INVESTMENT PERFORMANCE STANDARDS (GIPS®)

FOR ASSET OWNERS

2020

CFA Institute®
Global Investment
Performance Standards

ISBN 978-1-942713-72-2

CONTENTS

PREFACE

CFA Institute is a global not-for-profit association of investment professionals with the mission of leading the investment profession globally by setting the highest standards of ethics, education, and professional excellence. CFA Institute has a longstanding history of commitment to establishing and supporting the Global Investment Performance Standards (GIPS®). The GIPS standards are ethical standards for calculating and presenting investment performance based on the principles of fair representation and full disclosure.

The GIPS standards are the recognized standard for calculating and presenting investment performance around the world. Compliance with the GIPS standards has become a firm's "passport" to market investment management services globally. Asset owners that comply demonstrate a commitment to adhering to global best practices. As of June 2019, CFA Institute has partnered with organizations in more than 40 countries and regions that contribute to the development and promotion of the GIPS standards.

History

- In 1995, CFA Institute, formerly known as the Association for Investment Management and Research (AIMR), sponsored and funded the Global Investment Performance Standards Committee to develop global standards for calculating and presenting investment performance, based on the existing AIMR Performance Presentation Standards (AIMR-PPS®).

- The first Global Investment Performance Standards were published in April 1999. That year, the Global Investment Performance Standards Committee was replaced by the Investment Performance Council (IPC) to further develop and promote the GIPS standards. The development of the GIPS standards was a global industry initiative with participation from individuals and organizations from more than 15 countries.

- The IPC was charged with developing provisions for other asset classes (e.g., real estate and private equity) and addressing other performance-related issues (e.g., fees and advertising) to broaden the scope and applicability of the GIPS standards. The second edition of the GIPS standards, published in February 2005, accomplished this goal.

- With the 2005 edition release and the growing adoption and expansion of the GIPS standards, the IPC decided to move to a single global investment performance standard that would eliminate the need for local variations of the GIPS standards. All country-specific performance standards converged with the GIPS standards, resulting in 25 countries adopting a single, global standard for the calculation and presentation of investment performance.

 |

- In 2005, with the convergence of country-specific versions to the GIPS standards and the need to reorganize the governance structure to facilitate involvement from GIPS Standards Sponsors, CFA Institute dissolved the IPC and created the GIPS Executive Committee and the GIPS Council. The GIPS Executive Committee served as the decision-making authority for the GIPS standards, and the GIPS Council facilitated the involvement of all GIPS Standards Sponsors in the ongoing development and promotion of the GIPS standards.

- In 2008, the GIPS Executive Committee began a review of the GIPS standards in an effort to further refine the provisions. The GIPS Executive Committee collaborated closely with its technical subcommittees, specially formed working groups, and GIPS Standards Sponsors. These groups reviewed the existing provisions and guidance and conducted surveys and other research in the effort to produce the 2010 edition of the GIPS standards.

- In 2017, the GIPS Executive Committee concluded that the GIPS standards should better accommodate the needs of managers of pooled funds and alternative investments, as well as firms focusing on high-net-worth clients. In 2017, a Consultation Paper, which described the proposed key concepts of the GIPS standards and requested feedback on specific issues, was issued for public comment. The public comments received generally supported the proposed concepts. Subsequently, the 2020 GIPS Standards Exposure Draft was released on 31 August 2018. The final version of the 2020 edition of the GIPS standards was issued on 30 June 2019.

- The GIPS standards were originally created for investment firms managing composite strategies, with a focus on how firms present performance of composites to prospective clients. Asset owners, who were always able to claim compliance if they had discretion over their assets, struggled to understand how the GIPS standards applied to them. To address asset owners' needs, in 2014 the Guidance Statement on the Application of the GIPS Standards to Asset Owners was issued. This Guidance Statement explained how the requirements of the GIPS standards did or did not apply to asset owners. In the 2020 edition, separate provisions were created so that firms and asset owners each have provisions designed for them. Firms and those asset owners that market their services must follow the GIPS Standards for Firms. Asset owners that do not market their services will follow the GIPS Standards for Asset Owners. The GIPS Standards for Verifiers explain the procedures a verifier must follow when conducting a verification or performance examination.

INTRODUCTION

Preamble—Why Is a Global Investment Performance Standard Needed?

Standardize Investment Performance: Financial markets and the investment management industry have become increasingly global in nature. The growth in the types and number of financial entities, the globalization of the investment process, and the increased competition among investment management firms all demonstrate the need to standardize the calculation and presentation of investment performance.

Global Passport: Asset managers and both existing and prospective clients benefit from an established global standard for calculating and presenting investment performance. Investment practices, regulation, performance measurement, and reporting of performance vary considerably from country to country. By adhering to a global standard, firms in countries with minimal or no investment performance standards can compete for business on an equal footing with firms from countries with more-developed standards. Firms from countries with established practices can have more confidence in being fairly compared with local firms when competing for business in countries that have not previously adopted performance standards. Performance standards that are accepted globally enable investment firms to measure and present their investment performance so that investors can readily compare investment performance among firms.

Investor Confidence: Organizations that adhere to investment performance standards help assure investors and beneficiaries that the firm's and the asset owner's investment performance is complete and fairly presented. Both prospective and existing clients of investment firms as well as asset owner oversight bodies benefit from a global investment performance standard by having a greater degree of confidence in the performance information presented to them.

Mission and Objectives

The mission of the GIPS standards is to promote ethics and integrity and instill trust through the use of the GIPS standards by achieving universal demand for compliance by asset owners, adoption by asset managers, and support from regulators for the ultimate benefit of the global investment community.

 |

The objectives of the GIPS standards are as follows:

- Promote investor interests and instill investor confidence.
- Ensure accurate and consistent data.
- Obtain worldwide acceptance of a single standard for calculating and presenting performance.
- Promote fair, global competition among investment firms.
- Promote industry self-regulation on a global basis.

Overview

Key concepts of the GIPS standards that apply to asset owners include the following:

- The GIPS standards are ethical standards for investment performance presentation to ensure fair representation and full disclosure of investment performance.
- Meeting the objectives of fair representation and full disclosure is likely to require more than simply adhering to the minimum requirements of the GIPS standards. Asset owners should also adhere to the recommendations to achieve best practice in the calculation and presentation of performance.
- Asset owners must comply with all applicable requirements of the GIPS standards, including any Guidance Statements, interpretations, and Questions & Answers (Q&As) published by CFA Institute and the GIPS standards governing bodies.
- The GIPS standards do not address every aspect of performance measurement and will continue to evolve over time to address additional areas of investment performance.
- Asset owners must maintain and provide to their oversight bodies information about all of the total funds they manage. This provides oversight bodies with important information that allows them to make investment decisions and evaluate performance. Asset owners may also create additional composites and present asset class returns in a GIPS Asset Owner Report, which allows even more insight into their investment strategies.
- The GIPS standards rely on the integrity of input data, the quality of which is critical to creating accurate performance presentations. The underlying valuations of portfolio holdings drive performance. It is essential for these and other inputs to be accurate. The GIPS standards require asset owners to adhere to certain calculation methodologies and to make specific disclosures along with the asset owner's performance.

Historical Performance Record

An asset owner is required to initially present, at a minimum, one year of annual investment performance that is compliant with the GIPS standards. If the total fund or composite has been in existence less than one year, the asset owner must present performance since the total fund or composite inception date.

After an asset owner presents a minimum of one year of GIPS-compliant performance (or for the period since the total fund or composite inception date if the total fund or composite has been in existence less than one year), the asset owner must present an additional year of performance each year, building up to a minimum of 10 years of GIPS-compliant performance. The asset owner must include only GIPS-compliant performance in GIPS Asset Owner Reports. This requirement does not preclude asset owners from presenting longer track records that link GIPS-compliant performance to non-GIPS-compliant performance, but this linking must be done outside of GIPS Asset Owner Reports.

Claiming Compliance and Verification

Asset owners must take all steps necessary to ensure that they have satisfied all the applicable requirements of the GIPS standards before claiming compliance. Asset owners are strongly encouraged to perform periodic internal compliance checks. Implementing adequate internal controls during all stages of the investment performance process—from data input to preparing GIPS Asset Owner Reports—instills confidence in the validity of performance presented as well as in the claim of compliance.

Asset owners may choose to have an independent third-party verification. Verification is a process by which a verification firm (verifier) conducts testing of an asset owner on an asset owner–wide basis, in accordance with the required verification procedures of the GIPS standards. Verification provides assurance on whether the asset owner's policies and procedures related to total fund and composite maintenance, as well as the calculation, presentation, and distribution of performance, have been designed in compliance with the GIPS standards and if they have been implemented on an asset owner–wide basis. The value of verification is widely recognized, and being verified is considered to be best practice. It is recommended that asset owners be verified. In addition to verification, asset owners may also choose to have specifically focused testing of a total fund or composite (performance examination) performed by an independent third-party verifier to provide additional assurance regarding the performance of a particular total fund or composite.

  |

Implementing a Global Standard

One objective of the GIPS standards is to obtain worldwide acceptance of a single standard for the calculation and presentation of investment performance in a fair and comparable format that provides full disclosure. To facilitate the implementation of the GIPS standards, CFA Institute, together with the GIPS standards governing bodies, creates and administers the GIPS standards while local GIPS Standards Sponsors help to promote them.

Countries without an investment performance standard are strongly encouraged to promote the GIPS standards as the local standard and translate them into the local language when necessary. Although the GIPS standards may be translated into many languages, if a discrepancy arises, the English version of the GIPS standards is the official governing version.

The self-regulatory nature of the GIPS standards necessitates a strong commitment to ethical integrity. Self-regulation also assists regulators in exercising their responsibility for ensuring the fair disclosure of information within financial markets. Regulators are encouraged to do the following:

- Recognize the benefit of voluntary compliance with standards that represent global best practices;
- Consider taking enforcement action against asset owners that falsely claim compliance with the GIPS standards; and
- Recognize the value of and encourage independent third-party verification.

Where existing laws, regulations, or industry standards already impose requirements related to the calculation and presentation of investment performance, asset owners are strongly encouraged to comply with the GIPS standards in addition to applicable regulatory requirements. Compliance with applicable laws and regulations does not necessarily lead to compliance with the GIPS standards. In cases in which laws and/or regulations conflict with the GIPS standards, asset owners are required to comply with the laws and regulations and make full disclosure of the conflict in the GIPS Asset Owner Report.

GIPS Standards Sponsors

The presence of a local GIPS Standards Sponsor is essential for effective implementation of the GIPS standards and ongoing support within a country or region. Working in partnership with CFA Institute, GIPS Standards Sponsors play a key role in promoting the GIPS standards globally. GIPS Standards Sponsors, composed of one or more industry organizations, provide an important link between their local markets and the GIPS standards governing bodies. In addition to delivering educational programs and promoting the GIPS standards across the local investment profession, the GIPS Standards Sponsors own any CFA Institute-approved translation of the GIPS standards materials and are responsible for protecting it.

x | www.cfainstitute.org

Endorsed GIPS Standards Sponsors (as of 30 June 2019)

Australia
Financial Services Council (FSC)

Canada
Canadian Investment Performance Council
(CIPC)

China
CFA Society Beijing

Cyprus
CFA Society Cyprus

Czech Republic
CFA Society Czech Republic and Czech
Capital Market Association (AKAT)

Denmark
CFA Society Denmark and The Danish Finance
Society

France
CFA Society France and Association Française
de la Gestion Financière (AFG)

Germany
German Asset Management Standards
Committee (GAMSC):
Bundesverband Investment und Asset
Manager e.V. (BVI); Deutsche Vereinigung fur
Finanzanalyse und Assetment Management
(DVFA); and CFA Society Germany

Ghana
Ghana Securities Industry Association (GSIA)

Greece
CFA Society Greece

India
CFA Society India

Indonesia
CFA Society Indonesia and Indonesia
Association of Mutual Fund Managers
(Asosiasi Pengelola Reksa Dana Indonesia,
or APRDI)

Ireland
Irish Association of Investment Managers
(IAIM)

Italy
Italian Investment Performance Committee
(IIPC):
Associazione Bancaria Italiana (ABI);
Associazione Italiana degli Analisti
e Consulenti Finanziari (AIAF); Assogestioni;
Società per lo sviluppo del Mercato dei
Fondi Pensione (Mefop); Associazione
Italiana Revisori Contabili (Assirevi);
and CFA Society Italy

Japan
The Securities Analysts Association of Japan
(SAAJ)

Kazakhstan
Association of Financial and Investment
Analysts (AFIA)

Korea
Korea Investment Performance Committee
(KIPC)

Liechtenstein
Liechtenstein Bankers Association (LBA)

Mexico
CFA Society Mexico

Micronesia
Asia Pacific Association for Fiduciary Studies
(APAFS)

The Netherlands
VBA-Beleggingsprofessionals

New Zealand
CFA Society New Zealand

Nigeria
Nigeria Investment Performance Committee: CFA Society Nigeria; Pensions Operators Association of Nigeria (PENOP); and Fund Managers Association of Nigeria (FMAN)

Norway
The Norwegian Society of Financial Analysts (NFF)

Pakistan
CFA Society Pakistan

Peru
Procapitales

Philippines
CFA Society Philippines; Fund Managers Association of the Philippines (FMAP); and Trust Officers Association of the Philippines (TOAP)

Poland
CFA Society Poland

Portugal
Associação Portuguesa de Analista Financeiros (APAF)

Russia
CFA Association Russia

Saudi Arabia
CFA Society Saudi Arabia

Singapore
Investment Management Association of Singapore (IMAS)

South Africa
Association for Savings and Investment South Africa (ASISA)

Spain
Asociación Española de Presentación de Resultados de Gestión

Sri Lanka
CFA Society Sri Lanka

Sweden
CFA Society Sweden and The Swedish Society of Financial Analysts (Sveriges Finansanalytikers Forening, or SFF)

Switzerland
Swiss Funds & Asset Management Association (SFAMA)

Thailand
The Association of Provident Fund (AOP)

Ukraine
The Ukrainian Association of Investment Business (UAIB)

United Kingdom
United Kingdom Investment Performance Committee (UKIPC):
The Investment Association (TIA);
The Association of British Insurers (ABI);
Pensions and Lifetime Savings Association (PLSA); The Association of Consulting Actuaries (ACA); The Society of Pension Consultants (SPC); The Investment Property Forum (IPF); The Alternative Investment Management Association (AIMA); and The Wealth Management Association (WMA)

United States
United States Investment Performance Committee (USIPC) of CFA Institute

Provisions of the Global Investment Performance Standards

The 2020 Edition of the GIPS Standards has three chapters:

1) GIPS Standards for Firms
2) GIPS Standards for Asset Owners
3) GIPS Standards for Verifiers

The GIPS Standards for Asset Owners are for asset owners that do not compete for business and that report their performance to an oversight body. Asset owners that compete for business must comply with the GIPS Standards for Firms.

The GIPS Standards for Asset Owners are divided into the following six sections:

21) **Fundamentals of Compliance:** Several core principles create the foundation for the GIPS standards, including properly defining the asset owner, providing GIPS Asset Owner Reports to those who have direct oversight responsibility for total fund assets and total asset owner assets, adhering to applicable laws and regulations, and ensuring that information presented is not false or misleading. Two important issues that an asset owner must consider when becoming compliant with the GIPS standards are the definition of the asset owner and the asset owner's responsibility to present relevant information to its oversight body. The definition of the asset owner is the foundation for asset owner–wide compliance and creates defined boundaries whereby total asset owner assets can be determined. The oversight body has direct responsibility for total fund assets and total asset owner assets. The quality of the decisions it makes is based on the quality of information it receives.

22) **Input Data and Calculation Methodology:** Consistency of input data used to calculate performance is critical to effective compliance with the GIPS standards and establishes the foundation for full and fair investment performance presentations. Achieving transparency among asset owner's performance presentations requires uniformity in methods used to calculate returns. The GIPS standards mandate the use of certain calculation methodologies to facilitate a clear understanding of the information. It is important that the data being presented to the oversight body is consistent and transparent to aid in the evaluation of performance information and foster strong investment decision-making.

23) **Total Fund and Composite Maintenance:** A total fund is a pool of assets managed by an asset owner according to a specific investment mandate, which is typically composed of multiple asset classes. The total fund is typically composed of underlying portfolios, each representing one of the strategies used to achieve the asset owner's investment mandate. The asset owner is required to create a total fund and present total fund information to the oversight body.

 |

A composite is an aggregation of one or more portfolios managed according to a similar investment mandate, objective, or strategy. The composite return is the asset-weighted average of the performance of all portfolios in the composite. Asset owners are not required to present composites in compliance with the GIPS standards but may choose to do so. If an asset owner chooses to create an additional composite and present it in a GIPS Asset Owner Report, it must present the GIPS Asset Owner Report to the oversight body.

Reporting Sections: Two sections detail asset owners' reporting requirements and recommendations:

24) Total Fund and Composite Time-Weighted Return Report

25) Additional Composite Money-Weighted Return Report.

Asset owners are required to present time-weighted returns for total funds and must prepare GIPS Asset Owner Reports that include all of the requirements from Section 24. Asset owners may also include money-weighted returns in GIPS Asset Owner Reports for total funds but are not required to do so. Asset owners that choose to create and report additional composites in compliance with the GIPS standards may choose to present either time-weighted returns or money-weighted returns. Each reporting section is self-contained and includes all requirements and recommendations relevant to that particular report.

After identifying all total funds, constructing any additional composites, gathering the input data, and calculating returns, the asset owner must incorporate this information in GIPS Asset Owner Reports. No finite set of requirements can cover all potential situations or anticipate future developments in investment industry structure, technology, products, or practices. When appropriate, asset owners have the responsibility to include in GIPS Asset Owner Reports information not addressed by the GIPS standards.

Disclosures allow asset owners to elaborate on the data provided in the presentation and give the reader the proper context in which to understand the performance. To comply with the GIPS standards, an asset owner must disclose certain information in all GIPS Asset Owner Reports regarding its performance and related policies. Although some disclosures are required for all asset owners, others are specific to certain circumstances and may not apply in all situations. Asset owners are not required to make negative assurance disclosures (e.g., if the asset owner does not use leverage in a particular total fund, no disclosure about the use of leverage is required). One of the essential disclosures for every asset owner is the claim of compliance. Once an asset owner meets all the applicable requirements of the GIPS standards, it must appropriately use the claim of compliance to indicate compliance with the GIPS standards. Asset owners are also required to submit a GIPS Compliance Notification Form to CFA Institute when they initially claim compliance and on an annual basis thereafter.

26) GIPS Advertising Guidelines: Asset owners may wish to prepare materials that are widely distributed, such as annual reports provided to beneficiaries and posted on the asset owner's website. The asset owner may wish to include the fact that the asset owner claims compliance with the GIPS standards but does not wish to include a lengthy GIPS Asset Owner Report for the total fund. The asset owner may instead choose to prepare these materials following the GIPS Advertising Guidelines. To claim compliance with the GIPS standards in an advertisement, asset owners must adhere to the GIPS Advertising Guidelines or include a GIPS Asset Owner Report.

Glossary: Words appearing in small capital letters in Sections 21–26 are defined terms. The Glossary includes a description of each defined term.

Appendices: The appendices include samples of GIPS Asset Owner Reports, a list of total fund and composite descriptions, and a GIPS Advertisement.

 |

EFFECTIVE DATE

The effective date for the 2020 edition of the GIPS standards is 1 January 2020. GIPS Asset Owner Reports that include performance for periods ending on or after 31 December 2020 must be prepared in accordance with the 2020 edition of the GIPS standards. Prior editions of the GIPS standards may be found on the CFA Institute website (www.cfainstitute.org).

21. FUNDAMENTALS OF COMPLIANCE

21.A. Fundamentals of Compliance—Requirements

21.A.1   The GIPS standards MUST be applied on an ASSET OWNER–wide basis. Compliance MUST be met on an ASSET OWNER–wide basis and cannot be met on a TOTAL FUND, COMPOSITE, POOLED FUND, or PORTFOLIO basis.

21.A.2   An ASSET OWNER MUST be defined as an entity that manages investments, directly and/or through the use of EXTERNAL MANAGERS, on behalf of participants, beneficiaries, or the organization itself. These entities include, but are not limited to, public and private pension funds, endowments, foundations, family offices, provident funds, insurers and reinsurers, sovereign wealth funds, and fiduciaries.

21.A.3   The ASSET OWNER MUST have discretion over TOTAL FUND assets, either by managing assets directly or by having the discretion to hire and fire EXTERNAL MANAGERS.

21.A.4   To initially claim compliance with the GIPS standards, an ASSET OWNER MUST attain compliance for a minimum of one year or for the period since the ASSET OWNER inception if the ASSET OWNER has been in existence for less than one year.

21.A.5   The ASSET OWNER MUST comply with all applicable REQUIREMENTS of the GIPS standards, including any Guidance Statements, interpretations, and Questions & Answers (Q&As) published by CFA Institute and the GIPS standards governing bodies.

21.A.6   The ASSET OWNER MUST:

   a.   Document its policies and procedures used in establishing and maintaining compliance with the REQUIREMENTS of the GIPS standards, as well as any RECOMMENDATIONS it has chosen to adopt, and apply them consistently.

   b.   Create policies and procedures to monitor and identify changes and additions to all of the Guidance Statements, interpretations, and Q&As published by CFA Institute and the GIPS standards governing bodies.

21.A.7   The ASSET OWNER MUST:

   a.   Comply with all applicable laws and regulations regarding the calculation and presentation of performance.

   b.   Create policies and procedures to monitor and identify changes and additions to laws and regulations regarding the calculation and presentation of performance.

21.A.8   The ASSET OWNER MUST NOT present performance or PERFORMANCE-RELATED INFORMATION that is false or misleading. This REQUIREMENT applies to all performance or PERFORMANCE-RELATED INFORMATION on an ASSET OWNER–wide basis and is not limited to those materials that reference the GIPS standards. The ASSET OWNER may provide any performance or PERFORMANCE-RELATED INFORMATION that is specifically requested by the OVERSIGHT BODY.

21.A.9 If the ASSET OWNER does not meet all the applicable REQUIREMENTS of the GIPS standards, the ASSET OWNER MUST NOT represent or state that it is "in compliance with the Global Investment Performance Standards except for…" or make any other statements that may indicate compliance or partial compliance with the GIPS standards.

21.A.10 Statements referring to the calculation methodology as being "in accordance," "in compliance," or "consistent" with the Global Investment Performance Standards, or similar statements, are prohibited.

21.A.11 The ASSET OWNER MUST:

    a. Provide a GIPS ASSET OWNER REPORT for all TOTAL FUNDS and any additional COMPOSITES that have been created to the OVERSIGHT BODY.

    b. Provide an updated GIPS ASSET OWNER REPORT for all TOTAL FUNDS and any additional COMPOSITES that have been created to the OVERSIGHT BODY at least once every 12 months.

21.A.12 The ASSET OWNER may provide a GIPS ASSET OWNER REPORT to those who have a more indirect fiduciary role but is not REQUIRED to do so.

21.A.13 When providing GIPS ASSET OWNER REPORTS to an OVERSIGHT BODY, the ASSET OWNER MUST update these reports to include information through the most recent annual period end within 12 months of that annual period end.

21.A.14 The ASSET OWNER MUST be able to demonstrate how it provided GIPS ASSET OWNER REPORTS to the OVERSIGHT BODY.

21.A.15 A BENCHMARK used in a GIPS ASSET OWNER REPORT MUST reflect the investment mandate, objective, or strategy of the TOTAL FUND or COMPOSITE. The ASSET OWNER MUST NOT use a price-only BENCHMARK in a GIPS ASSET OWNER REPORT.

21.A.16 The ASSET OWNER MUST correct MATERIAL ERRORS in GIPS ASSET OWNER REPORTS and MUST:

    a. Provide the corrected GIPS ASSET OWNER REPORT to the current verifier.

    b. Provide the corrected GIPS ASSET OWNER REPORT to any former verifiers that received the GIPS ASSET OWNER REPORT that had the MATERIAL ERROR.

    c. Provide the corrected GIPS ASSET OWNER REPORT to any OVERSIGHT BODY that received the GIPS ASSET OWNER REPORT that had the MATERIAL ERROR.

21.A.17 The ASSET OWNER MUST maintain a complete list of TOTAL FUND DESCRIPTIONS and COMPOSITE DESCRIPTIONS for any COMPOSITE that has been presented in a GIPS ASSET OWNER REPORT. The ASSET OWNER MUST include terminated TOTAL FUNDS and COMPOSITES on this list for at least five years after the TOTAL FUND TERMINATION DATE or COMPOSITE TERMINATION DATE. If the ASSET OWNER has only one REQUIRED TOTAL FUND and has not chosen to create any additional COMPOSITES, the GIPS ASSET OWNER REPORT for the TOTAL FUND may be used.

21.A.18 The ASSET OWNER MUST provide the complete list of TOTAL FUND DESCRIPTIONS and COMPOSITE DESCRIPTIONS to the OVERSIGHT BODY if it makes such a request. If the ASSET OWNER has only one REQUIRED TOTAL FUND and has not chosen to create any additional COMPOSITES, the GIPS ASSET OWNER REPORT for the TOTAL FUND may be used.

21.A.19 All data and information necessary to support all items included in GIPS ASSET OWNER REPORTS and GIPS ADVERTISEMENTS MUST be captured, maintained, and available within a reasonable time frame, for all periods presented in these reports and advertisements.

21.A.20 The ASSET OWNER is responsible for its claim of compliance with the GIPS standards and MUST ensure that the records and information provided by any third party on which the ASSET OWNER relies meet the REQUIREMENTS of the GIPS standards.

21.A.21 The ASSET OWNER MUST NOT LINK actual performance to historical THEORETICAL PERFORMANCE.

21.A.22 Changes in an ASSET OWNER's organization MUST NOT lead to alteration of historical performance.

21.A.23 The ASSET OWNER MUST NOT present non-GIPS-compliant performance in GIPS ASSET OWNER REPORTS.

21.A.24 If an ASSET OWNER competes for business, the ASSET OWNER MUST follow all sections of the GIPS Standards for Firms and all applicable REQUIREMENTS when competing for business.

21.A.25 The ASSET OWNER MUST present TIME-WEIGHTED RETURNS for all TOTAL FUNDS. The ASSET OWNER may present MONEY-WEIGHTED RETURNS in addition to TIME-WEIGHTED RETURNS for TOTAL FUNDS.

21.A.26 The ASSET OWNER MUST choose to present TIME-WEIGHTED RETURNS, MONEY-WEIGHTED RETURNS, or both for each additional COMPOSITE and MUST consistently present the selected returns for each additional COMPOSITE.

21.A.27 The ASSET OWNER MUST notify CFA Institute of its claim of compliance by submitting the GIPS COMPLIANCE NOTIFICATION FORM. This form:

   a. MUST be filed when the ASSET OWNER initially claims compliance with the GIPS standards.

   b. MUST be updated annually with information as of the most recent 31 December, with the exception of ASSET OWNER contact information, which MUST be current as of the form submission date.

   c. MUST be filed annually thereafter by 30 June.

21.A.28 If an ASSET OWNER chooses to be verified, it MUST gain an understanding of the verifier's policies for maintaining independence and MUST consider the verifier's assessment of independence.

21.B. Fundamentals of Compliance—Recommendations

21.B.1 The ASSET OWNER SHOULD comply with the RECOMMENDATIONS of the GIPS standards, including RECOMMENDATIONS in any Guidance Statements, interpretations, and Q&As published by CFA Institute and the GIPS standards governing bodies.

21.B.2 The ASSET OWNER SHOULD update GIPS ASSET OWNER REPORTS quarterly.

21.B.3 The ASSET OWNER SHOULD be verified.

22. INPUT DATA AND CALCULATION METHODOLOGY

22.A. Input Data and Calculation Methodology—Requirements

Assets

22.A.1 TOTAL ASSET OWNER ASSETS MUST be the aggregate FAIR VALUE of all discretionary and non-discretionary assets managed by the ASSET OWNER. This includes both fee-paying and non-fee-paying PORTFOLIOS.[1]

22.A.2 TOTAL ASSET OWNER ASSETS, TOTAL FUND assets, and COMPOSITE assets MUST:

    a. Include only actual assets managed by the ASSET OWNER.

    b. Be calculated net of leverage and not grossed up as if the leverage did not exist.

22.A.3 The ASSET OWNER MUST NOT double count assets when calculating TOTAL ASSET OWNER ASSETS, TOTAL FUND assets, and COMPOSITE assets.

22.A.4 TOTAL FUND and COMPOSITE performance MUST be calculated using only actual assets managed by the ASSET OWNER.

General/Accounting

22.A.5 TOTAL RETURNS MUST be used.

22.A.6 TRADE DATE ACCOUNTING MUST be used.[2]

22.A.7 ACCRUAL ACCOUNTING MUST be used for fixed-income securities and all other investments that earn interest income, except that interest income on cash and cash equivalents may be recognized on a cash basis. Any accrued income MUST be included in the beginning and ending TOTAL FUND and PORTFOLIO values when performance is calculated.

22.A.8 Cash and cash equivalents that are considered discretionary and part of the investable assets of the TOTAL FUND MUST be included in TOTAL FUND assets and performance calculations.

22.A.9 Returns for periods of less than one year MUST NOT be annualized.

---

[1] REQUIRED for periods beginning on or after 1 January 2011. For periods prior to 1 January 2011, TOTAL ASSET OWNER ASSETS MUST be the aggregate of either the FAIR VALUE or the MARKET VALUE of all discretionary and non-discretionary assets managed by the ASSET OWNER.

[2] REQUIRED for periods beginning on or after 1 January 2005.

22.A.10 All returns MUST be calculated after the deduction of TRANSACTION COSTS incurred during the period. The ASSET OWNER may use estimated TRANSACTION COSTS only for those PORTFOLIOS for which actual TRANSACTION COSTS are not known.

22.A.11 For PORTFOLIOS with BUNDLED FEES, if the ASSET OWNER cannot estimate TRANSACTION COSTS or if actual TRANSACTION COSTS cannot be segregated from a BUNDLED FEE, when calculating GROSS-OF-FEES returns or NET-OF-EXTERNAL-COSTS-ONLY returns, these returns MUST be reduced by the entire BUNDLED FEE or the portion of the BUNDLED FEE that includes the TRANSACTION COSTS.

22.A.12 All REQUIRED returns MUST be calculated net of leverage.

22.A.13 The ASSET OWNER MUST calculate performance in accordance with its TOTAL FUND–specific or COMPOSITE-specific calculation policies.

22.A.14 For an ASSET OWNER invested in underlying POOLED FUNDS, all returns MUST reflect the deduction of all fees and expenses charged at the underlying POOLED FUND level.

22.A.15 When calculating ADDITIONAL RISK MEASURES:

    a. The PERIODICITY of the TOTAL FUND or COMPOSITE returns and the BENCHMARK returns MUST be the same.

    b. The risk measure calculation methodology of the TOTAL FUND or COMPOSITE and the BENCHMARK MUST be the same.

Valuation

22.A.16 TOTAL FUNDS and PORTFOLIOS MUST be valued in accordance with the definition of FAIR VALUE.[3]

22.A.17 The ASSET OWNER MUST value TOTAL FUNDS and PORTFOLIOS in accordance with the TOTAL FUND–specific or COMPOSITE-specific valuation policy.

22.A.18 If the ASSET OWNER uses the last available historical price or preliminary, estimated value as FAIR VALUE, the ASSET OWNER MUST:

    a. Consider it to be the best approximation of the current FAIR VALUE.

    b. Assess the difference between the approximation and final value and the effect on TOTAL FUND assets or COMPOSITE assets, TOTAL ASSET OWNER ASSETS, and performance, and also make any adjustments when the final value is received.

22.A.19 TOTAL FUNDS and COMPOSITES MUST have consistent beginning and ending annual valuation dates. Unless the TOTAL FUND or COMPOSITE is reported on a non-calendar fiscal

---

[3] REQUIRED for periods beginning on or after 1 January 2011. For periods prior to 1 January 2011, PORTFOLIO valuations (excluding REAL ESTATE and PRIVATE EQUITY) MUST be based on FAIR VALUES or MARKET VALUES. For periods prior to 1 January 2011, REAL ESTATE investments MUST be valued at FAIR VALUE or MARKET VALUE (as previously defined for REAL ESTATE in the 2005 edition of the GIPS standards). For periods ending prior to 1 January 2011, PRIVATE EQUITY investments MUST be valued at FAIR VALUE, according to either the GIPS Private Equity Valuation Principles in Appendix D of the 2005 version of the GIPS standards or the GIPS Valuation Principles in Chapter II of the 2010 edition of the GIPS standards.

year, the beginning and ending valuation dates MUST be at calendar year end or on the last business day of the year.[4]

Time-Weighted Returns

22.A.20 When calculating TIME-WEIGHTED RETURNS, TOTAL FUNDS and PORTFOLIOS except PRIVATE MARKET INVESTMENT PORTFOLIOS (see 22.A.30) MUST be valued:

    a. At least monthly.[5]

    b. As of the calendar month end or the last business day of the month.[6]

    c. On the date of all LARGE CASH FLOWS. The ASSET OWNER MUST define LARGE CASH FLOW for each TOTAL FUND and COMPOSITE to determine when the TOTAL FUND and PORTFOLIOS in a COMPOSITE MUST be valued.[7]

22.A.21 When calculating TIME-WEIGHTED RETURNS for TOTAL FUNDS and PORTFOLIOS except PRIVATE MARKET INVESTMENT PORTFOLIOS (see 22.A.31), the ASSET OWNER MUST:

    a. Calculate returns at least monthly.[8]

    b. Calculate monthly returns through the calendar month end or the last business day of the month.[9]

    c. Calculate sub-period returns at the time of all LARGE CASH FLOWS, if daily returns are not calculated.[10]

    d. For EXTERNAL CASH FLOWS that are not LARGE CASH FLOWS, calculate TOTAL FUND and PORTFOLIO returns that adjust for daily-weighted EXTERNAL CASH FLOWS, if daily returns are not calculated.[11]

    e. Treat EXTERNAL CASH FLOWS according to the TOTAL FUND–specific or COMPOSITE-specific policy.

    f. Geometrically LINK periodic and sub-period returns.

    g. Consistently apply the calculation methodology used for an individual TOTAL FUND or PORTFOLIO.

---

[4] REQUIRED for periods beginning on or after 1 January 2006.

[5] REQUIRED for periods beginning on or after 1 January 2001. For periods prior to 1 January 2001, PORTFOLIOS MUST be valued at least quarterly.

[6] REQUIRED for periods beginning on or after 1 January 2010.

[7] REQUIRED for periods beginning on or after 1 January 2010.

[8] REQUIRED for periods beginning on or after 1 January 2001.

[9] REQUIRED for periods beginning on or after 1 January 2010.

[10] REQUIRED for periods beginning on or after 1 January 2010.

[11] REQUIRED for periods beginning on or after 1 January 2005.

 |

Money-Weighted Returns

22.A.22 When calculating MONEY-WEIGHTED RETURNS, the ASSET OWNER MUST value PORTFOLIOS at least annually and as of the period end for any period for which performance is calculated.

22.A.23 When calculating MONEY-WEIGHTED RETURNS, the ASSET OWNER MUST:

    a. Calculate annualized SINCE-INCEPTION MONEY-WEIGHTED RETURNS or the annualized MONEY-WEIGHTED RETURN for the longest period for which the ASSET OWNER has sufficient records.

    b. Calculate MONEY-WEIGHTED RETURNS using daily EXTERNAL CASH FLOWS.[12]

    c. Include stock DISTRIBUTIONS as EXTERNAL CASH FLOWS and value stock DISTRIBUTIONS at the time of DISTRIBUTION.

Gross and Net Returns

22.A.24 When the ASSET OWNER calculates TOTAL FUND and COMPOSITE NET-OF-FEES returns, these returns MUST reflect the deduction of:[13]

    a. TRANSACTION COSTS.

    b. All fees and expenses for externally managed POOLED FUNDS.

    c. INVESTMENT MANAGEMENT FEES for externally managed SEGREGATED ACCOUNTS.

    d. INVESTMENT MANAGEMENT COSTS.

22.A.25 When the ASSET OWNER calculates TOTAL FUND and COMPOSITE NET-OF-EXTERNAL-COSTS-ONLY returns, these returns MUST reflect the deduction of:[14]

    a. TRANSACTION COSTS.

    b. All fees and expenses for externally managed POOLED FUNDS.

    c. INVESTMENT MANAGEMENT FEES for externally managed SEGREGATED ACCOUNTS.

22.A.26 When the ASSET OWNER calculates TOTAL FUND and COMPOSITE GROSS-OF-FEES returns, these returns MUST reflect the deduction of:[15]

    a. TRANSACTION COSTS.

    b. All fees and expenses for externally managed POOLED FUNDS.

---

[12] Daily EXTERNAL CASH FLOWS are REQUIRED beginning 1 January 2020. Prior to 1 January 2020, quarterly or more frequent EXTERNAL CASH FLOWS MUST be used.

[13] REQUIRED for periods beginning on or after 1 January 2015.

[14] REQUIRED for periods beginning on or after 1 January 2015.

[15] REQUIRED for periods beginning on or after 1 January 2015.

Composite Returns

22.A.27 Composite time-weighted returns except private market investment composites (see 22.A.32) must be calculated at least monthly.[16]

22.A.28 Composite time-weighted returns must be calculated by using one of the following approaches:

   a. Asset-weighting the individual portfolio returns using beginning-of-period values;

   b. Asset-weighting the individual portfolio returns using a method that reflects both beginning-of-period values and external cash flows; or

   c. Using the aggregate method.

22.A.29 When calculating composite money-weighted returns, the asset owner must calculate composite returns by aggregating the portfolio-level information for those portfolios included in the composite.

Private Market Investments

22.A.30 When calculating time-weighted returns for private market investment portfolios that are included in composites, private market investment portfolios must be valued:

   a. At least quarterly.[17]

   b. As of each quarter end or the last business day of the quarter.[18]

22.A.31 When calculating time-weighted returns for private market investment portfolios that are included in composites, the asset owner must:

   a. Calculate returns at least quarterly.[19]

   b. Calculate quarterly returns through the calendar quarter end or the last business day of the quarter.[20]

   c. Calculate portfolio returns that adjust for daily-weighted external cash flows.[21]

   d. Treat external cash flows according to the asset owner's composite-specific policy.

   e. Geometrically link periodic and sub-period returns.

   f. Consistently apply the calculation methodology used for an individual portfolio.

---

[16] Required for periods beginning on or after 1 January 2010. For periods beginning on or after 1 January 2006 and ending prior to 1 January 2010, composite returns must be calculated at least quarterly.

[17] Required for periods beginning on or after 1 January 2008.

[18] Required for periods beginning on or after 1 January 2010.

[19] Required for periods beginning on or after 1 January 2008.

[20] Required for periods beginning on or after 1 January 2010.

[21] Required for periods beginning on or after 1 January 2010.

22.A.32 Composite time-weighted returns for private market investment composites must be calculated at least quarterly.

Real Estate

22.A.33 Real estate investments that are directly owned by the asset owner must:[22]

    a. Have an external valuation at least once every 12 months unless the oversight body stipulates otherwise, in which case real estate investments must have an external valuation at least once every 36 months or per oversight body instructions if the oversight body requires external valuations more frequently than every 36 months; or

    b. Be subject to an annual financial statement audit performed by an independent public accounting firm. The real estate investments must be accounted for at fair value and the most recent audited financial statements available must contain an unmodified opinion issued by an independent public accounting firm.

22.A.34 External valuations for real estate investments must be performed by an independent third party who is a professionally designated or certified commercial property valuer or appraiser. In markets where these professionals are not available, the asset owner must take necessary steps to ensure that only qualified independent property valuers or appraisers are used.

22.A.35 The asset owner must not use external valuations for real estate investments when the valuer's or appraiser's fee is contingent upon the investment's appraised value.

Side Pockets

22.A.36 All total fund, composite, and pooled fund returns must include the effect of any side pockets held by total funds, portfolios, or pooled funds.

22.B. Input Data and Calculation Methodology—Recommendations

22.B.1 The asset owner should value total funds and portfolios on the date of all external cash flows.

22.B.2 Valuations should be obtained from a qualified independent third party.

22.B.3 Accrual accounting should be used for dividends (as of the ex-dividend date).

22.B.4 The asset owner should accrue investment management fees and investment management costs.

---

[22] Required for periods beginning on or after 1 January 2012.

22.B.5 Returns SHOULD be calculated net of non-reclaimable withholding taxes on dividends, interest, and capital gains. Reclaimable withholding taxes SHOULD be accrued.

22.B.6 The ASSET OWNER SHOULD incorporate the following hierarchy into its policies and procedures for determining FAIR VALUE for PORTFOLIO investments on a TOTAL FUND–specific or COMPOSITE-specific basis.

    a. Investments MUST be valued using objective, observable, unadjusted quoted market prices for identical investments in active markets on the measurement date, if available. If such prices are not available, then investments SHOULD be valued using;

    b. Objective, observable quoted market prices for similar investments in active markets. If such prices are not available or appropriate, then investments SHOULD be valued using;

    c. Quoted prices for identical or similar investments in markets that are not active (markets in which there are few transactions for the investment, the prices are not current, or price quotations vary substantially over time and/or between market makers). If such prices are not available or appropriate, then investments SHOULD be valued based on;

    d. Market-based inputs, other than quoted prices, that are observable for the investment. If such prices are not available or appropriate, then investments SHOULD be valued based on;

    e. Subjective, unobservable inputs for the investment where markets are not active at the measurement date. Unobservable inputs SHOULD be used to measure FAIR VALUE only when observable inputs and prices are not available or appropriate. Unobservable inputs reflect the ASSET OWNER'S own assumptions about the assumptions that market participants would use in pricing the investment and SHOULD be developed based on the best information available under the circumstances.

22.B.7 The ASSET OWNER SHOULD use GROSS-OF-FEES returns when calculating risk measures.

22.B.8 PRIVATE MARKET INVESTMENTS SHOULD have an EXTERNAL VALUATION at least once every 12 months.

22.B.9 Operating cash accounts that are not fully available for investment SHOULD NOT be included in TOTAL ASSET OWNER ASSETS, TOTAL FUND assets, or COMPOSITE assets.

22.B.10 Operating cash accounts that are not fully available for investment SHOULD NOT be included in TOTAL FUND returns or COMPOSITE returns.

| **11**

23. TOTAL FUND AND COMPOSITE MAINTENANCE

23.A. Total Fund and Composite Maintenance—Requirements

23.A.1 TOTAL FUNDS MUST include all assets managed by the ASSET OWNER as part of the TOTAL FUND's investment mandate, objective, or strategy.

23.A.2 If the ASSET OWNER manages more than one TOTAL FUND according to the same strategy, all TOTAL FUNDS managed according to the same investment strategy MUST be presented either:[23]

    a. Separately to the OVERSIGHT BODY, or

    b. As a COMPOSITE to the OVERSIGHT BODY.

23.A.3 If the ASSET OWNER manages TOTAL FUNDS according to different strategies, then each TOTAL FUND MUST be presented separately to the OVERSIGHT BODY.

23.A.4 COMPOSITES MUST be defined according to investment mandate, objective, or strategy. COMPOSITES MUST include all PORTFOLIOS that meet the COMPOSITE DEFINITION. If the ASSET OWNER chooses to create an additional COMPOSITE, then all PORTFOLIOS that meet the COMPOSITE DEFINITION MUST be included in the additional COMPOSITE.

23.A.5 Any change to a COMPOSITE DEFINITION MUST NOT be applied retroactively.

23.A.6 TOTAL FUNDS and COMPOSITES MUST include new PORTFOLIOS on a timely and consistent basis as soon as they are funded.

23.A.7 Terminated PORTFOLIOS MUST be included in the historical performance of the TOTAL FUND or COMPOSITE through the final day the assets are managed.

23.A.8 If the ASSET OWNER chooses to create a COMPOSITE that includes more than one TOTAL FUND, or if the ASSET OWNER creates additional COMPOSITES, TOTAL FUNDS and PORTFOLIOS MUST NOT be moved from one COMPOSITE to another unless either (1) documented ASSET OWNER–directed changes to a TOTAL FUND's or PORTFOLIO's investment mandate, objective, or strategy or (2) the redefinition of the COMPOSITE make it appropriate. The historical performance of the TOTAL FUND or PORTFOLIO MUST remain with the original COMPOSITE. TOTAL FUNDS and PORTFOLIOS MUST NOT be moved into or out of COMPOSITES as a result of tactical changes.

---

[23] REQUIRED for periods beginning on or after 1 January 2015.

 www.cfainstitute.org

24. TOTAL FUND AND COMPOSITE TIME-WEIGHTED RETURN REPORT

The following provisions apply to ASSET OWNERS that include TIME-WEIGHTED RETURNS in a GIPS ASSET OWNER REPORT.

24.A. Presentation and Reporting—Requirements

24.A.1   The ASSET OWNER MUST present in each GIPS ASSET OWNER REPORT:

a. At least one year of performance (or for the period since the TOTAL FUND or COMPOSITE INCEPTION DATE if the TOTAL FUND or COMPOSITE has been in existence less than one year) that meets the REQUIREMENTS of the GIPS standards. After the ASSET OWNER presents a minimum of one year of GIPS-compliant performance (or for the period since the TOTAL FUND or COMPOSITE INCEPTION DATE if the TOTAL FUND or COMPOSITE has been in existence less than one year), the ASSET OWNER MUST present an additional year of performance each year, building up to a minimum of 10 years of GIPS-compliant performance.

b. For TOTAL FUNDS, TOTAL FUND returns that are NET-OF-FEES.[24]

c. TOTAL FUND or COMPOSITE returns for each annual period.

d. When the initial period is less than a full year, the return from the TOTAL FUND or COMPOSITE INCEPTION DATE through the initial annual period end.[25]

e. When the TOTAL FUND or COMPOSITE terminates, the return from the last annual period end through the TOTAL FUND TERMINATION DATE or COMPOSITE TERMINATION DATE.[26]

f. The TOTAL RETURN for the BENCHMARK for each annual period and for all other periods for which TOTAL FUND or COMPOSITE returns are presented, unless the ASSET OWNER determines there is no appropriate BENCHMARK.

g. The number of TOTAL FUNDS or PORTFOLIOS in the COMPOSITE as of each annual period end.[27]

---

[24] REQUIRED for periods beginning on or after 1 January 2015.

[25] REQUIRED for COMPOSITES with a COMPOSITE INCEPTION DATE of 1 January 2011 or later.

[26] REQUIRED for COMPOSITES with a COMPOSITE TERMINATION DATE of 1 January 2011 or later.

[27] REQUIRED for periods ending on or after 31 December 2020. For periods ending prior to 31 December 2020, if the COMPOSITE contains five or fewer PORTFOLIOS at period end, the number of PORTFOLIOS is not REQUIRED.

h. TOTAL FUND assets or COMPOSITE assets as of each annual period end.

i. TOTAL ASSET OWNER ASSETS as of each annual period end.[28]

j. For TOTAL FUNDS or COMPOSITES for which monthly TOTAL FUND or COMPOSITE returns are available, the three-year annualized EX POST STANDARD DEVIATION (using monthly returns) of the TOTAL FUND or COMPOSITE and the BENCHMARK as of each annual period end.[29]

24.A.2 The ASSET OWNER MUST present the percentage of the total FAIR VALUE of TOTAL FUND assets or COMPOSITE assets that were valued using subjective unobservable inputs (as described in provision 22.B.6) as of the most recent annual period end, if such investments represent a material amount of TOTAL FUND assets or COMPOSITE assets.

24.A.3 The ASSET OWNER MUST clearly label or identify:

a. The periods that are presented.

b. If returns presented are GROSS-OF-FEES, NET-OF-EXTERNAL-COSTS-ONLY, or NET-OF-FEES.

24.A.4 If the ASSET OWNER presents FULL GROSS-OF-FEES RETURNS, the ASSET OWNER MUST identify them as SUPPLEMENTAL INFORMATION.

24.A.5 If the ASSET OWNER includes more than one BENCHMARK in the GIPS ASSET OWNER REPORT, the ASSET OWNER MUST present and disclose all REQUIRED information for all BENCHMARKS presented.

24.A.6 If the COMPOSITE loses all of its member PORTFOLIOS, the COMPOSITE track record MUST end. If PORTFOLIOS are later added to the COMPOSITE, the COMPOSITE track record MUST restart. The periods both before and after the break in track record MUST be presented, with the break in performance clearly shown. The ASSET OWNER MUST NOT LINK performance prior to the break in track record to the performance after the break in track record.

24.A.7 All REQUIRED and RECOMMENDED information in the GIPS ASSET OWNER REPORT MUST be presented in the same currency.

24.A.8 Any SUPPLEMENTAL INFORMATION included in the GIPS ASSET OWNER REPORT:

a. MUST relate directly to the TOTAL FUND or COMPOSITE.

b. MUST NOT contradict or conflict with the REQUIRED or RECOMMENDED information in the GIPS ASSET OWNER REPORT.

c. MUST be clearly labeled as SUPPLEMENTAL INFORMATION.

---

[28] REQUIRED for periods ending on or after 31 December 2020. For periods ending prior to 31 December 2020, the ASSET OWNER may present either TOTAL ASSET OWNER ASSETS or TOTAL FUND assets or COMPOSITE assets as a percentage of TOTAL ASSET OWNER ASSETS.

[29] REQUIRED for periods ending on or after 1 January 2011.

24.B. Presentation and Reporting—Recommendations

24.B.1   The ASSET OWNER SHOULD present GROSS-OF-FEES and NET-OF-EXTERNAL-COSTS-ONLY TOTAL FUND returns.

24.B.2   The ASSET OWNER SHOULD present GROSS-OF-FEES, NET-OF-EXTERNAL-COSTS-ONLY, and NET-OF-FEES COMPOSITE returns.

24.B.3   The ASSET OWNER SHOULD present the following items:

    a. Cumulative returns of the TOTAL FUND or COMPOSITE and the BENCHMARK for all periods.

    b. Equal-weighted COMPOSITE returns.

    c. Quarterly and/or monthly returns.

    d. Annualized TOTAL FUND or COMPOSITE and BENCHMARK returns for periods longer than 12 months.

24.B.4   The ASSET OWNER SHOULD present MONEY-WEIGHTED RETURNS for TOTAL FUNDS when the ASSET OWNER believes MONEY-WEIGHTED RETURNS are helpful and important in understanding the performance of the TOTAL FUND.

24.B.5   For all periods for which an annualized EX POST STANDARD DEVIATION of the TOTAL FUND or COMPOSITE and the BENCHMARK are presented, the ASSET OWNER SHOULD present the corresponding annualized return of the TOTAL FUND or COMPOSITE and the BENCHMARK.

24.B.6   For all periods greater than three years for which an annualized return of the TOTAL FUND or COMPOSITE and the BENCHMARK are presented, the ASSET OWNER SHOULD present the corresponding annualized EX POST STANDARD DEVIATION (using monthly returns) of the TOTAL FUND or COMPOSITE and the BENCHMARK.

24.B.7   The ASSET OWNER SHOULD present relevant EX POST ADDITIONAL RISK MEASURES for the TOTAL FUND or COMPOSITE and the BENCHMARK.

24.B.8   The ASSET OWNER SHOULD present more than 10 years of annual performance in the GIPS ASSET OWNER REPORT.

24.B.9   If the ASSET OWNER uses preliminary, estimated values as FAIR VALUE, the ASSET OWNER SHOULD present the percentage of assets in the TOTAL FUND or COMPOSITE that were valued using preliminary, estimated values as of each annual period end.

24.B.10 For REAL ESTATE COMPOSITES, the ASSET OWNER SHOULD present COMPOSITE and BENCHMARK COMPONENT RETURNS for all periods presented.

 |

24.C. Disclosure–Requirements

24.C.1 Once the ASSET OWNER has met all the applicable REQUIREMENTS of the GIPS standards, the ASSET OWNER MUST disclose its compliance with the GIPS standards using one of the following compliance statements. The compliance statement MUST only be used in a GIPS ASSET OWNER REPORT.

a.   For an ASSET OWNER that is verified:

"[Insert name of ASSET OWNER] claims compliance with the Global Investment Performance Standards (GIPS®) and has prepared and presented this report in compliance with the GIPS standards. [Insert name of ASSET OWNER] has been independently verified for the periods [insert dates]. The verification report(s) is/are available upon request.

"An asset owner that claims compliance with the GIPS standards must establish policies and procedures for complying with all the applicable requirements of the GIPS standards. Verification provides assurance on whether the asset owner's policies and procedures related to total fund and composite maintenance, as well as the calculation, presentation, and distribution of performance, have been designed in compliance with the GIPS standards and have been implemented on an asset owner–wide basis. Verification does not provide assurance on the accuracy of any specific performance report."

b.   For TOTAL FUNDS or COMPOSITES of a verified ASSET OWNER that have also had a PERFORMANCE EXAMINATION:

"[Insert name of ASSET OWNER] claims compliance with the Global Investment Performance Standards (GIPS®) and has prepared and presented this report in compliance with the GIPS standards. [Insert name of ASSET OWNER] has been independently verified for the periods [insert dates].

"An asset owner that claims compliance with the GIPS standards must establish policies and procedures for complying with all the applicable requirements of the GIPS standards. Verification provides assurance on whether the asset owner's policies and procedures related to total fund and composite maintenance, as well as the calculation, presentation, and distribution of performance, have been designed in compliance with the GIPS standards and have been implemented on an asset owner–wide basis. The [insert name of TOTAL FUND or COMPOSITE] has had a performance examination for the periods [insert dates]. The verification and performance examination reports are available upon request."

The compliance statement for an ASSET OWNER that is verified or for TOTAL FUNDS or COMPOSITES of a verified ASSET OWNER that have also had a PERFORMANCE EXAMINATION is complete only when both paragraphs are shown together, one after the other.

c. For an ASSET OWNER that has not been verified:

"[Insert name of ASSET OWNER] claims compliance with the Global Investment Performance Standards (GIPS®) and has prepared and presented this report in compliance with the GIPS standards. [Insert name of ASSET OWNER] has not been independently verified."

The ASSET OWNER MUST NOT exclude any portion of the respective compliance statement. Any modifications to the compliance statement MUST be additive.

24.C.2 The ASSET OWNER MUST disclose the following: "GIPS® is a registered trademark of CFA Institute. CFA Institute does not endorse or promote this organization, nor does it warrant the accuracy or quality of the content contained herein."

24.C.3 The ASSET OWNER MUST disclose the definition of the ASSET OWNER used to determine TOTAL ASSET OWNER ASSETS and ASSET OWNER–wide compliance.

24.C.4 The ASSET OWNER MUST disclose the TOTAL FUND DESCRIPTION or COMPOSITE DESCRIPTION.

24.C.5 The ASSET OWNER MUST disclose:

a. The BENCHMARK DESCRIPTION, which MUST include the key features of the BENCHMARK or the name of the BENCHMARK for a readily recognized index or other point of reference.

b. The PERIODICITY of the BENCHMARK if BENCHMARK returns are calculated less frequently than monthly.

24.C.6 When presenting GROSS-OF-FEES returns, the ASSET OWNER MUST disclose if any other fees are deducted in addition to TRANSACTION COSTS and fees and expenses for externally managed POOLED FUNDS.

24.C.7 When presenting NET-OF-EXTERNAL-COSTS-ONLY returns, the ASSET OWNER MUST disclose if any other fees are deducted in addition to the TRANSACTION COSTS, fees and expenses for externally managed POOLED FUNDS, and INVESTMENT MANAGEMENT FEES for externally managed SEGREGATED ACCOUNTS.

24.C.8 When presenting COMPOSITE NET-OF-FEES returns, the ASSET OWNER MUST disclose if any other fees are deducted in addition to the TRANSACTION COSTS, fees and expenses for externally managed POOLED FUNDS, INVESTMENT MANAGEMENT FEES for externally managed SEGREGATED ACCOUNTS, and INVESTMENT MANAGEMENT COSTS.

24.C.9 The ASSET OWNER MUST disclose or otherwise indicate the reporting currency.

24.C.10 The ASSET OWNER MUST disclose the TOTAL FUND INCEPTION DATE or COMPOSITE INCEPTION DATE.

24.C.11 For COMPOSITES, the ASSET OWNER MUST disclose the COMPOSITE CREATION DATE.

24.C.12 If the ASSET OWNER chooses to create additional COMPOSITES, or if the ASSET OWNER has more than one REQUIRED TOTAL FUND, the ASSET OWNER MUST disclose that the ASSET

OWNER's list of TOTAL FUND DESCRIPTIONS and COMPOSITE DESCRIPTIONS is available upon request.

24.C.13 The ASSET OWNER MUST disclose that policies for valuing investments, calculating performance, and preparing GIPS ASSET OWNER REPORTS are available upon request.

24.C.14 The ASSET OWNER MUST disclose how leverage, derivatives, and short positions have been used historically, if material.

24.C.15 If estimated TRANSACTION COSTS are used, the ASSET OWNER MUST disclose:

    a. That estimated TRANSACTION COSTS were used.

    b. The estimated TRANSACTION COSTS used and how they were determined.

24.C.16 The ASSET OWNER MUST disclose all significant events that would help the OVERSIGHT BODY interpret the GIPS ASSET OWNER REPORT. This disclosure MUST be included for a minimum of one year and for as long as it is relevant to interpreting the track record.

24.C.17 If the ASSET OWNER is redefined, the ASSET OWNER MUST disclose the date and description of the redefinition.

24.C.18 If a COMPOSITE is redefined, the ASSET OWNER MUST disclose the date and description of the redefinition.

24.C.19 The ASSET OWNER MUST disclose changes to the name of a TOTAL FUND or COMPOSITE. This disclosure MUST be included for a minimum of one year and for as long as it is relevant to interpreting the track record.

24.C.20 The ASSET OWNER MUST disclose if TOTAL FUND or COMPOSITE returns are gross or net of withholding taxes, if material.

24.C.21 The ASSET OWNER MUST disclose if BENCHMARK returns are net of withholding taxes if this information is available.

24.C.22 If the GIPS ASSET OWNER REPORT conforms with laws and/or regulations that conflict with the REQUIREMENTS of the GIPS standards, the ASSET OWNER MUST disclose this fact and disclose the manner in which the laws and/or regulations conflict with the GIPS standards.

24.C.23 The ASSET OWNER MUST disclose the use of EXTERNAL MANAGERS and the periods EXTERNAL MANAGERS were used.[30]

24.C.24 The ASSET OWNER MUST disclose if the TOTAL FUND's or COMPOSITE's valuation hierarchy materially differs from the RECOMMENDED valuation hierarchy.[31] (See provision 22.B.6 for the RECOMMENDED valuation hierarchy.)

24.C.25 If the ASSET OWNER determines no appropriate BENCHMARK for the TOTAL FUND or COMPOSITE exists, the ASSET OWNER MUST disclose why no BENCHMARK is presented.

---

[30] REQUIRED for periods beginning on or after 1 January 2006.

[31] REQUIRED for periods beginning on or after 1 January 2011.

24.C.26 If the ASSET OWNER changes the BENCHMARK, the ASSET OWNER MUST disclose:

    a. For a prospective BENCHMARK change, the date and description of the change. Changes MUST be disclosed for as long as returns for the prior BENCHMARK are included in the GIPS ASSET OWNER REPORT.

    b. For a retroactive BENCHMARK change, the date and description of the change. Changes MUST be disclosed for a minimum of one year and for as long as they are relevant to interpreting the track record.

24.C.27 If a custom BENCHMARK or combination of multiple BENCHMARKS is used, the ASSET OWNER MUST:

    a. Disclose the BENCHMARK components, weights, and rebalancing process, if applicable.

    b. Disclose the calculation methodology.

    c. Clearly label the BENCHMARK to indicate that it is a custom BENCHMARK.

24.C.28 If the TOTAL FUND BENCHMARK is a blend of asset class BENCHMARKS based on the policy weights of the respective asset classes, the ASSET OWNER MUST disclose:

    a. The BENCHMARKS used by each asset class along with their weights as of the most recent annual period end.

    b. General information regarding the investments, structure, and/or characteristics of the BENCHMARKS.

24.C.29 If a PORTFOLIO-WEIGHTED CUSTOM BENCHMARK is used, the ASSET OWNER MUST disclose:

    a. That the BENCHMARK is rebalanced using the weighted average returns of the BENCHMARKS of all of the PORTFOLIOS included in the COMPOSITE.

    b. The frequency of the rebalancing.

    c. The components that constitute the PORTFOLIO-WEIGHTED CUSTOM BENCHMARK, including the weights that each component represents, as of the most recent annual period end.

    d. That the components that constitute the PORTFOLIO-WEIGHTED CUSTOM BENCHMARK, including the weights that each component represents, are available for prior periods upon request.

24.C.30 For TOTAL FUNDS and COMPOSITES with at least three annual periods of performance, the ASSET OWNER MUST disclose if the three-year annualized EX POST STANDARD DEVIATION of the TOTAL FUND or COMPOSITE and/or BENCHMARK is not presented because 36 monthly returns are not available.

24.C.31 The ASSET OWNER MUST disclose any change to the GIPS ASSET OWNER REPORT resulting from the correction of a MATERIAL ERROR. Following the correction of the GIPS ASSET OWNER REPORT, this disclosure MUST be included for a minimum of one year and for as long as it is relevant to interpreting the track record.

 |

24.C.32 The ASSET OWNER MUST disclose if preliminary, estimated values are used to determine FAIR VALUE.

24.C.33 If the ASSET OWNER changes the type of return(s) presented for the COMPOSITE (e.g., changes from MONEY-WEIGHTED RETURNS to TIME-WEIGHTED RETURNS), the ASSET OWNER MUST disclose the change and the date of the change. This disclosure MUST be included for a minimum of one year and for as long as it is relevant to interpreting the track record.

24.C.34 If the ASSET OWNER presents ADDITIONAL RISK MEASURES, the ASSET OWNER MUST:

    a. Describe any ADDITIONAL RISK MEASURE.

    b. Disclose the name of the risk-free rate if a risk-free rate is used in the calculation of the ADDITIONAL RISK MEASURE.

24.C.35 The ASSET OWNER MUST disclose if GROSS-OF-FEES, NET-OF-EXTERNAL-COSTS-ONLY, or NET-OF-FEES returns are used to calculate presented risk measures.

24.C.36 For REAL ESTATE investments that are directly owned, the ASSET OWNER MUST disclose that:[32]

    a. EXTERNAL VALUATIONS are obtained and the frequency with which they are obtained; or

    b. The ASSET OWNER relies on valuations from financial statement audits.

24.C.37 When the GIPS ASSET OWNER REPORT includes THEORETICAL PERFORMANCE as SUPPLEMENTAL INFORMATION, the ASSET OWNER MUST:

    a. Disclose that the results are theoretical, are not based on the performance of actual assets, and if the THEORETICAL PERFORMANCE was derived from the retroactive or prospective application of a model.

    b. Disclose a basic description of the methodology and assumptions used to calculate the THEORETICAL PERFORMANCE sufficient for the OVERSIGHT BODY to interpret the THEORETICAL PERFORMANCE, including if it is based on model performance, backtested performance, or hypothetical performance.

    c. Disclose whether the THEORETICAL PERFORMANCE reflects the deduction of actual or estimated INVESTMENT MANAGEMENT FEES, INVESTMENT MANAGEMENT COSTS, and TRANSACTION COSTS.

    d. Clearly label the THEORETICAL PERFORMANCE as SUPPLEMENTAL INFORMATION.

---

[32] REQUIRED for periods ending on or after 31 December 2020.

24.D. Disclosure—Recommendations

24.D.1   The ASSET OWNER SHOULD disclose material changes to valuation policies and/or methodologies.

24.D.2   The ASSET OWNER SHOULD disclose material changes to calculation policies and/or methodologies.

24.D.3   The ASSET OWNER SHOULD disclose material differences between the BENCHMARK and the TOTAL FUND'S or COMPOSITE'S investment mandate, objective, or strategy.

24.D.4   The ASSET OWNER SHOULD disclose the key assumptions used to value investments.

24.D.5   If the ASSET OWNER adheres to any industry valuation guidelines in addition to the GIPS valuation REQUIREMENTS, the ASSET OWNER SHOULD disclose which guidelines have been applied.

24.D.6   When using BENCHMARKS that have limitations, such as peer group BENCHMARKS, the ASSET OWNER SHOULD disclose these limitations.

24.D.7   The ASSET OWNER SHOULD disclose information about the INVESTMENT MANAGEMENT FEES and INVESTMENT MANAGEMENT COSTS of the TOTAL FUND or COMPOSITE that were incurred during the most recent annual period.

25. ADDITIONAL COMPOSITE MONEY-WEIGHTED RETURN REPORT

The following provisions apply to ASSET OWNERS that calculate and report additional COMPOSITE performance in a GIPS ASSET OWNER REPORT using MONEY-WEIGHTED RETURNS.

25.A. Presentation and Reporting—Requirements

25.A.1. The ASSET OWNER MUST present in each GIPS ASSET OWNER REPORT:

    a. The annualized COMPOSITE SINCE-INCEPTION MONEY-WEIGHTED RETURN through the most recent annual period end. If the ASSET OWNER has no records to support this track record, the ASSET OWNER MUST present the ANNUALIZED MONEY-WEIGHTED RETURN for the longest period for which the ASSET OWNER has such records, through the most recent annual period end.

    b. When the COMPOSITE has a track record that is less than a full year, the non-annualized COMPOSITE SINCE-INCEPTION MONEY-WEIGHTED RETURN or the COMPOSITE non-annualized MONEY-WEIGHTED RETURN for the longest period for which the ASSET OWNER has records through the initial annual period end.

    c. When the COMPOSITE terminates, the annualized COMPOSITE SINCE-INCEPTION MONEY-WEIGHTED RETURN through the COMPOSITE TERMINATION DATE or the COMPOSITE annualized MONEY-WEIGHTED RETURN for the longest period for which the ASSET OWNER has records through the COMPOSITE TERMINATION DATE.

    d. The MONEY-WEIGHTED RETURN for the BENCHMARK for the same periods as presented for the COMPOSITE, unless the ASSET OWNER determines there is no appropriate BENCHMARK.

    e. The number of PORTFOLIOS in the COMPOSITE as of the most recent annual period end.[33]

    f. COMPOSITE assets as of the most recent annual period end.

    g. TOTAL ASSET OWNER ASSETS as of the most recent annual period end.[34]

---

[33] REQUIRED for periods ending on or after 31 December 2020. For periods ending prior to 31 December 2020, if the COMPOSITE contains five or fewer PORTFOLIOS at period end, the number of PORTFOLIOS is not REQUIRED.

[34] REQUIRED for periods ending on or after 31 December 2020. For periods ending prior to 31 December 2020, ASSET OWNERS may present either TOTAL ASSET OWNER ASSETS or COMPOSITE assets as a percentage of TOTAL ASSET OWNER ASSETS.

25.A.2 The ASSET OWNER MUST present the percentage of the total FAIR VALUE of COMPOSITE assets that were valued using subjective unobservable inputs (as described in provision 22.B.6) as of the most recent annual period end, if such investments represent a material amount of COMPOSITE assets.

25.A.3 For COMPOSITES where the underlying PORTFOLIOS have COMMITTED CAPITAL, the ASSET OWNER MUST present the following items as of the most recent annual period end:

  a. COMPOSITE SINCE-INCEPTION PAID-IN CAPITAL.

  b. COMPOSITE SINCE-INCEPTION DISTRIBUTIONS.

  c. COMPOSITE cumulative COMMITTED CAPITAL.

  d. TOTAL VALUE to SINCE-INCEPTION PAID-IN CAPITAL (INVESTMENT MULTIPLE or TVPI).

  e. SINCE-INCEPTION DISTRIBUTIONS to SINCE-INCEPTION PAID-IN CAPITAL (REALIZATION MULTIPLE or DPI).

  f. SINCE-INCEPTION PAID-IN CAPITAL to cumulative COMMITTED CAPITAL (PIC MULTIPLE).

  g. RESIDUAL VALUE to SINCE-INCEPTION PAID-IN CAPITAL (UNREALIZED MULTIPLE or RVPI).

25.A.4 The ASSET OWNER MUST clearly label or identify:

  a. The periods that are presented.

  b. If returns presented are GROSS-OF-FEES, NET-OF-EXTERNAL-COSTS-ONLY, or NET-OF-FEES.

25.A.5 If the ASSET OWNER presents FULL GROSS-OF-FEES RETURNS, the ASSET OWNER MUST identify them as SUPPLEMENTAL INFORMATION.

25.A.6 If the ASSET OWNER includes more than one BENCHMARK in the GIPS ASSET OWNER REPORT, the ASSET OWNER MUST present and disclose all REQUIRED information for all BENCHMARKS presented.

25.A.7 All REQUIRED and RECOMMENDED information in the GIPS ASSET OWNER REPORT MUST be presented in the same currency.

25.A.8 Any SUPPLEMENTAL INFORMATION included in the GIPS ASSET OWNER REPORT:

  a. MUST relate directly to the COMPOSITE.

  b. MUST NOT contradict or conflict with the REQUIRED or RECOMMENDED information in the GIPS ASSET OWNER REPORT.

  c. MUST be clearly labeled as SUPPLEMENTAL INFORMATION.

 |

25.B. Presentation and Reporting–Recommendations

25.B.1 The ASSET OWNER SHOULD present SINCE-INCEPTION MONEY-WEIGHTED RETURNS as of each annual period end.

25.B.2 For COMPOSITES where the underlying PORTFOLIOS have COMMITTED CAPITAL, the ASSET OWNER SHOULD present the following items as of each annual period end:

   a. COMPOSITE SINCE-INCEPTION PAID-IN CAPITAL.

   b. COMPOSITE SINCE-INCEPTION DISTRIBUTIONS.

   c. COMPOSITE cumulative COMMITTED CAPITAL.

   d. TOTAL VALUE TO SINCE-INCEPTION PAID-IN CAPITAL (INVESTMENT MULTIPLE or TVPI).

   e. SINCE-INCEPTION DISTRIBUTIONS TO SINCE-INCEPTION PAID-IN CAPITAL (REALIZATION MULTIPLE or DPI).

   f. SINCE-INCEPTION PAID-IN CAPITAL to cumulative COMMITTED CAPITAL (PIC MULTIPLE).

   g. RESIDUAL VALUE TO SINCE-INCEPTION PAID-IN CAPITAL (UNREALIZED MULTIPLE or RVPI).

25.B.3 The ASSET OWNER SHOULD present GROSS-OF-FEES, NET-OF-EXTERNAL-COSTS-ONLY, and NET-OF-FEES COMPOSITE RETURNS.

25.B.4 The ASSET OWNER SHOULD present an appropriate EX POST risk measure for the COMPOSITE and the BENCHMARK. The same EX POST risk measure SHOULD be presented for the COMPOSITE and the BENCHMARK.

25.B.5 If the ASSET OWNER uses preliminary, estimated values as FAIR VALUE, the ASSET OWNER SHOULD present the percentage of assets in the COMPOSITE that were valued using preliminary, estimated values as of the most recent annual period end.

25.C. Disclosure–Requirements

25.C.1 Once the ASSET OWNER has met all the applicable REQUIREMENTS of the GIPS standards, the ASSET OWNER MUST disclose its compliance with the GIPS standards using one of the following compliance statements. The compliance statement for a COMPOSITE MUST only be used in a GIPS ASSET OWNER REPORT.

   a. For an ASSET OWNER that is verified:

   "[Insert name of ASSET OWNER] claims compliance with the Global Investment Performance Standards (GIPS®) and has prepared and presented this report in compliance with the GIPS standards. [Insert name of ASSET

OWNER] has been independently verified for the periods [insert dates]. The verification report(s) is/are available upon request.

"An asset owner that claims compliance with the GIPS standards must establish policies and procedures for complying with all the applicable requirements of the GIPS standards. Verification provides assurance on whether the asset owner's policies and procedures related to total fund and composite maintenance, as well as the calculation, presentation, and distribution of performance, have been designed in compliance with the GIPS standards and have been implemented on an asset owner–wide basis. Verification does not provide assurance on the accuracy of any specific performance report."

b. For COMPOSITES of a verified ASSET OWNER that have also had a PERFORMANCE EXAMINATION:

"[Insert name of ASSET OWNER] claims compliance with the Global Investment Performance Standards (GIPS®) and has prepared and presented this report in compliance with the GIPS standards. [Insert name of ASSET OWNER] has been independently verified for the periods [insert dates].

"An asset owner that claims compliance with the GIPS standards must establish policies and procedures for complying with all the applicable requirements of the GIPS standards. Verification provides assurance on whether the asset owner's policies and procedures related to total fund and composite maintenance, as well as the calculation, presentation, and distribution of performance, have been designed in compliance with the GIPS standards and have been implemented on an asset owner–wide basis. The [insert name of COMPOSITE] has had a performance examination for the periods [insert dates]. The verification and performance examination reports are available upon request."

The compliance statement for an ASSET OWNER that is verified, or for TOTAL FUNDS or COMPOSITES of a verified ASSET OWNER that have also had a PERFORMANCE EXAMINATION, is complete only when both paragraphs are shown together, one after the other.

c. For an ASSET OWNER that has not been verified:

"[Insert name of ASSET OWNER] claims compliance with the Global Investment Performance Standards (GIPS®) and has prepared and presented this report in compliance with the GIPS standards. [Insert name of ASSET OWNER] has not been independently verified."

The ASSET OWNER MUST NOT exclude any portion of the respective compliance statement. Any modifications to the compliance statement MUST be additive.

25.C.2 The ASSET OWNER MUST disclose the following: "GIPS® is a registered trademark of CFA Institute. CFA Institute does not endorse or promote this organization, nor does it warrant the accuracy or quality of the content contained herein."

25.C.3 The ASSET OWNER MUST disclose the definition of the ASSET OWNER used to determine TOTAL ASSET OWNER ASSETS and ASSET OWNER–wide compliance.

25.C.4 The ASSET OWNER MUST disclose the COMPOSITE DESCRIPTION.

25.C.5 The ASSET OWNER MUST disclose the BENCHMARK DESCRIPTION, which MUST include the key features of the BENCHMARK or the name of the BENCHMARK for a readily recognized index or other point of reference.

25.C.6 When presenting GROSS-OF-FEES returns, the ASSET OWNER MUST disclose if any other fees are deducted in addition to TRANSACTION COSTS and fees and expenses for externally managed POOLED FUNDS.

25.C.7 When presenting NET-OF-EXTERNAL-COSTS-ONLY returns, the ASSET OWNER MUST disclose if any other fees are deducted in addition to the TRANSACTION COSTS, fees and expenses for externally managed POOLED FUNDS, and INVESTMENT MANAGEMENT FEES for externally managed SEGREGATED ACCOUNTS.

25.C.8 When presenting NET-OF-FEES returns, the ASSET OWNER MUST disclose if any other fees are deducted in addition to the TRANSACTION COSTS, fees and expenses for externally managed POOLED FUNDS, INVESTMENT MANAGEMENT FEES for externally managed SEGREGATED ACCOUNTS, and INVESTMENT MANAGEMENT COSTS.

25.C.9 The ASSET OWNER MUST disclose or otherwise indicate the reporting currency.

25.C.10 The ASSET OWNER MUST disclose the COMPOSITE INCEPTION DATE.

25.C.11 The ASSET OWNER MUST disclose the COMPOSITE CREATION DATE.

25.C.12 If the ASSET OWNER chooses to create additional COMPOSITES, or if the ASSET OWNER has more than one REQUIRED TOTAL FUND, the ASSET OWNER MUST disclose that the ASSET OWNER's list of TOTAL FUND DESCRIPTIONS and COMPOSITE DESCRIPTIONS is available upon request.

25.C.13 The ASSET OWNER MUST disclose that policies for valuing investments, calculating performance, and preparing GIPS ASSET OWNER REPORTS are available upon request.

25.C.14 The ASSET OWNER MUST disclose how leverage, derivatives, and short positions have been used historically, if material.

25.C.15 If estimated TRANSACTION COSTS are used, the ASSET OWNER MUST disclose:

    a. That estimated TRANSACTION COSTS were used.

    b. The estimated TRANSACTION COSTS used and how they were determined.

25.C.16 The ASSET OWNER MUST disclose all significant events that would help the OVERSIGHT BODY interpret the GIPS ASSET OWNER REPORT. This disclosure MUST be included for a minimum of one year and for as long as it is relevant to interpreting the track record.

25.C.17 If the ASSET OWNER is redefined, the ASSET OWNER MUST disclose the date and description of the redefinition.

25.C.18 If a COMPOSITE is redefined, the ASSET OWNER MUST disclose the date and description of the redefinition.

25.C.19 The ASSET OWNER MUST disclose changes to the name of the COMPOSITE. This disclosure MUST be included for a minimum of one year and for as long as it is relevant to interpreting the track record.

25.C.20 The ASSET OWNER MUST disclose if COMPOSITE returns are gross or net of withholding taxes, if material.

25.C.21 The ASSET OWNER MUST disclose if BENCHMARK returns are net of withholding taxes if this information is available.

25.C.22 If the GIPS ASSET OWNER REPORT conforms with laws and/or regulations that conflict with the REQUIREMENTS of the GIPS standards, the ASSET OWNER MUST disclose this fact and disclose the manner in which the laws and/or regulations conflict with the GIPS standards.

25.C.23 The ASSET OWNER MUST disclose the use of EXTERNAL MANAGERS and the periods EXTERNAL MANAGERS were used.[35]

25.C.24 The ASSET OWNER MUST disclose if the COMPOSITE's valuation hierarchy materially differs from the RECOMMENDED valuation hierarchy.[36] (See provision 22.B.6 for the RECOMMENDED valuation hierarchy.)

25.C.25 If the ASSET OWNER determines no appropriate BENCHMARK for the COMPOSITE exists, the ASSET OWNER MUST disclose why no BENCHMARK is presented.

25.C.26 If the ASSET OWNER changes the BENCHMARK, the ASSET OWNER MUST disclose:

    a. For a prospective BENCHMARK change, the date and description of the change. Changes MUST be disclosed for as long as returns for the prior BENCHMARK are included in the GIPS ASSET OWNER REPORT.

    b. For a retroactive BENCHMARK change, the date and description of the change. Changes MUST be disclosed for a minimum of one year and for as long as they are relevant to interpreting the track record.

25.C.27 If a custom BENCHMARK or combination of multiple BENCHMARKS is used, the ASSET OWNER MUST:

    a. Disclose the BENCHMARK components, weights, and rebalancing process, if applicable.

    b. Disclose the calculation methodology.

    c. Clearly label the BENCHMARK to indicate that it is a custom BENCHMARK.

---

[35] REQUIRED for periods beginning on or after 1 January 2006.
[36] REQUIRED for periods beginning on or after 1 January 2011.

|

25.C.28 The ASSET OWNER MUST disclose the calculation methodology used for the BENCHMARK. If the ASSET OWNER presents the PUBLIC MARKET EQUIVALENT of the COMPOSITE as a BENCHMARK, the ASSET OWNER MUST disclose the index used to calculate the PUBLIC MARKET EQUIVALENT.

25.C.29 The ASSET OWNER MUST disclose the frequency of EXTERNAL CASH FLOWS used in the MONEY-WEIGHTED RETURN calculation if daily frequency was not used.

25.C.30 The ASSET OWNER MUST disclose any change to the GIPS ASSET OWNER REPORT resulting from the correction of a MATERIAL ERROR. Following the correction of the GIPS ASSET OWNER REPORT, this disclosure MUST be included for a minimum of one year and for as long as it is relevant to interpreting the track record.

25.C.31 The ASSET OWNER MUST disclose if preliminary, estimated values are used to determine FAIR VALUE.

25.C.32 If the ASSET OWNER changes the type of return(s) presented for the COMPOSITE (e.g., changes from TIME-WEIGHTED RETURNS to MONEY-WEIGHTED RETURNS), the ASSET OWNER MUST disclose the change and the date of the change. This disclosure MUST be included for a minimum of one year and for as long as it is relevant to interpreting the track record.

25.C.33 If the ASSET OWNER presents ADDITIONAL RISK MEASURES, the ASSET OWNER MUST:

    a. Describe any ADDITIONAL RISK MEASURE.

    b. Disclose the name of the risk-free rate if a risk-free rate is used in the calculation of the ADDITIONAL RISK MEASURE.

25.C.34 The ASSET OWNER MUST disclose if GROSS-OF-FEES, NET-OF-EXTERNAL-COSTS-ONLY, or NET-OF-FEES returns are used to calculate presented risk measures.

25.C.35 For REAL ESTATE investments that are directly owned, the ASSET OWNER MUST disclose that:[37]

    a. EXTERNAL VALUATIONS are obtained and the frequency with which they are obtained; or

    b. The ASSET OWNER relies on valuations from financial statement audits.

25.C.36 When the GIPS ASSET OWNER REPORT includes THEORETICAL PERFORMANCE as SUPPLEMENTAL INFORMATION, the ASSET OWNER MUST:

    a. Disclose that the results are theoretical, are not based on the performance of actual assets, and if the THEORETICAL PERFORMANCE was derived from the retroactive or prospective application of a model.

---

[37] REQUIRED for periods ending on or after 31 December 2020.

b. Disclose a basic description of the methodology and assumptions used to calculate the THEORETICAL PERFORMANCE sufficient for the OVERSIGHT BODY to interpret the THEORETICAL PERFORMANCE, including if it is based on model performance, back-tested performance, or hypothetical performance.

c. Disclose whether the THEORETICAL PERFORMANCE reflects the deduction of actual or estimated INVESTMENT MANAGEMENT FEES, INVESTMENT MANAGEMENT COSTS, and TRANSACTION COSTS.

d. Clearly label the THEORETICAL PERFORMANCE as SUPPLEMENTAL INFORMATION.

25.D. Disclosure–Recommendations

25.D.1   The ASSET OWNER SHOULD disclose material changes to valuation policies and/or methodologies.

25.D.2   The ASSET OWNER SHOULD disclose material changes to calculation policies and/or methodologies.

25.D.3   The ASSET OWNER SHOULD disclose material differences between the BENCHMARK and the COMPOSITE's investment mandate, objective, or strategy.

25.D.4   The ASSET OWNER SHOULD disclose the key assumptions used to value investments.

25.D.5   If the ASSET OWNER adheres to any industry valuation guidelines in addition to the GIPS valuation REQUIREMENTS, the ASSET OWNER SHOULD disclose which guidelines have been applied.

25.D.6   When using BENCHMARKS that have limitations, such as peer group BENCHMARKS, the ASSET OWNER SHOULD disclose these limitations.

25.D.7   The ASSET OWNER SHOULD disclose information about the INVESTMENT MANAGEMENT FEES and INVESTMENT MANAGEMENT COSTS of the COMPOSITE that were incurred during the most recent annual period.

26. GIPS ADVERTISING GUIDELINES

Purpose of the GIPS Advertising Guidelines

The GIPS Advertising Guidelines provide ASSET OWNERS with options for advertising when mentioning the ASSET OWNER's claim of compliance. The GIPS Advertising Guidelines do not replace the GIPS standards, nor do they absolve ASSET OWNERS from presenting GIPS ASSET OWNER REPORTS as REQUIRED by the GIPS standards. These guidelines apply only to ASSET OWNERS that already satisfy all the applicable REQUIREMENTS of the GIPS standards on an ASSET OWNER–wide basis and prepare an advertisement that adheres to the REQUIREMENTS of the GIPS Advertising Guidelines (a "GIPS ADVERTISEMENT"). ASSET OWNERS may also choose to include a GIPS ASSET OWNER REPORT in the advertisement.

Definitions

Advertisement

For the GIPS Advertising Guidelines for ASSET OWNERS, an advertisement includes any materials that are distributed to or designed for use in newspapers, magazines, ASSET OWNER brochures, letters, media, websites, or any other written or electronic material distributed to more than one party, and there is no contact between the ASSET OWNER and the reader of the advertisement.

GIPS Advertisement

A GIPS ADVERTISEMENT is an advertisement by a GIPS-compliant ASSET OWNER that adheres to the REQUIREMENTS of the GIPS Advertising Guidelines.

Relationship of the GIPS Advertising Guidelines to Regulatory Requirements

When preparing GIPS ADVERTISEMENTS, ASSET OWNERS MUST also adhere to all applicable laws and regulations governing advertisements. ASSET OWNERS are encouraged to seek legal or regulatory counsel because additional disclosures may be REQUIRED. In cases where applicable laws or regulations conflict with the REQUIREMENTS of the GIPS standards or the GIPS Advertising Guidelines, ASSET OWNERS are REQUIRED to comply with the laws or regulations.

Other Information

The GIPS ADVERTISEMENT may include other information beyond what is REQUIRED or RECOMMENDED under the GIPS Advertising Guidelines provided the information is shown with equal or lesser prominence relative to the information REQUIRED or RECOMMENDED by the GIPS Advertising Guidelines and the information does not conflict with the REQUIREMENTS or RECOMMENDATIONS of the GIPS standards or the GIPS Advertising Guidelines. ASSET OWNERS MUST adhere to the principles of fair representation and full disclosure when advertising and MUST NOT present performance or PERFORMANCE-RELATED INFORMATION that is false or misleading.

26.A. Fundamental Requirements of the GIPS Advertising Guidelines

26.A.1 The GIPS Advertising Guidelines apply only to ASSET OWNERS that already claim compliance with the GIPS standards.

26.A.2 An ASSET OWNER that chooses to claim compliance in a GIPS ADVERTISEMENT MUST comply with all applicable REQUIREMENTS of the GIPS Advertising Guidelines.

26.A.3 The ASSET OWNER MUST maintain all data and information necessary to support all items included in a GIPS ADVERTISEMENT.

26.A.4 Returns for periods of less than one year included in a GIPS ADVERTISEMENT MUST NOT be annualized.

26.A.5 TOTAL FUND or COMPOSITE returns included in a GIPS ADVERTISEMENT MUST be derived from the returns included in or that will be included in the corresponding GIPS ASSET OWNER REPORT.

26.A.6 Disclosures included in a GIPS ADVERTISEMENT for a TOTAL FUND or COMPOSITE MUST be consistent with the related disclosure included in the corresponding GIPS ASSET OWNER REPORT, unless the disclosure included in the GIPS ADVERTISEMENT is more current and has not yet been reflected in the corresponding GIPS ASSET OWNER REPORT.

26.A.7 BENCHMARK returns included in a GIPS ADVERTISEMENT MUST be TOTAL RETURNS.

26.A.8 The ASSET OWNER MUST clearly label or identify:

   a. The name of the COMPOSITE or TOTAL FUND for which the GIPS ADVERTISEMENT is prepared.

   b. The name of any BENCHMARK included in the GIPS ADVERTISEMENT.

   c. The periods that are presented in the GIPS ADVERTISEMENT.

26.A.9 Other information beyond what is REQUIRED or RECOMMENDED under the GIPS Advertising Guidelines (e.g., COMPOSITE or TOTAL FUND returns for additional periods)

MUST be presented with equal or lesser prominence relative to the information REQUIRED or RECOMMENDED by the GIPS Advertising Guidelines. This information MUST NOT conflict with the REQUIREMENTS or RECOMMENDATIONS of the GIPS standards or the GIPS Advertising Guidelines.

26.A.10 All REQUIRED and RECOMMENDED information in a GIPS ADVERTISEMENT MUST be presented in the same currency.

26.B. GIPS Advertisements That Do Not Include Performance

26.B.1 The ASSET OWNER MUST disclose the GIPS Advertising Guidelines compliance statement:

> "[Insert name of ASSET OWNER] claims compliance with the Global Investment Performance Standards (GIPS®)."

26.B.2 The ASSET OWNER MUST disclose the following: "GIPS® is a registered trademark of CFA Institute. CFA Institute does not endorse or promote this organization, nor does it warrant the accuracy or quality of the content contained herein."

26.B.3 The ASSET OWNER MUST disclose how a participant or beneficiary may obtain GIPS-compliant performance information for the ASSET OWNER'S strategies and products.

26.C. GIPS Advertisements for a Total Fund or Composite That Include Performance—Requirements

26.C.1 If TIME-WEIGHTED RETURNS are presented in the corresponding GIPS ASSET OWNER REPORT, the ASSET OWNER MUST present TOTAL FUND or COMPOSITE TOTAL RETURNS according to one of the following:

   a. One-, three-, and five-year annualized TOTAL FUND or COMPOSITE returns through the most recent period. If the TOTAL FUND or COMPOSITE has been in existence for less than five years, or the ASSET OWNER presents less than five years of performance in the corresponding GIPS ASSET OWNER REPORT, the ASSET OWNER MUST also present the annualized return that includes all periods presented in the corresponding GIPS ASSET OWNER REPORT.

   b. The period-to-date TOTAL FUND or COMPOSITE return in addition to one-, three-, and five-year annualized TOTAL FUND or COMPOSITE returns through the same period as presented in the corresponding GIPS ASSET OWNER REPORT. If the TOTAL FUND or COMPOSITE has been in existence for less than five years, or the ASSET OWNER presents less than five years of performance in the corresponding GIPS ASSET OWNER REPORT, the ASSET OWNER MUST also present the annualized return that includes all periods presented in the corresponding GIPS ASSET OWNER REPORT.

   c. The period-to-date TOTAL FUND or COMPOSITE return in addition to five years of annual TOTAL FUND or COMPOSITE returns (or for each annual period presented in the corresponding GIPS ASSET OWNER REPORT if less than five years). The annual returns MUST be calculated through the same period as presented in the corresponding GIPS ASSET OWNER REPORT.

   d. The annualized TOTAL FUND or COMPOSITE return for the total period that includes all periods presented in the corresponding GIPS ASSET OWNER REPORT, through either:

     i. The most recent period end, or

     ii. The most recent annual period end.

26.C.2 If MONEY-WEIGHTED RETURNS are presented in the corresponding GIPS ASSET OWNER REPORT, the ASSET OWNER MUST present the annualized (for periods longer than one year) or non-annualized (for periods less than one year) TOTAL FUND or COMPOSITE MONEY-WEIGHTED RETURN that has the same start date as presented in the GIPS ASSET OWNER REPORT, through either:

   a. The most recent period end, or

   b. The most recent annual period end.

26.C.3 The ASSET OWNER MUST clearly label TOTAL FUND or COMPOSITE returns as GROSS-OF-FEES, NET-OF-EXTERNAL-COSTS-ONLY, or NET-OF-FEES.

26.C.4 The ASSET OWNER MUST present BENCHMARK returns for the same BENCHMARK as presented in the corresponding GIPS ASSET OWNER REPORT, if the corresponding GIPS ASSET OWNER REPORT includes BENCHMARK returns. BENCHMARK returns MUST be of the same return type (TIME-WEIGHTED RETURNS or MONEY-WEIGHTED RETURNS), in the same currency, and for the same periods for which the TOTAL FUND or COMPOSITE returns are presented.

26.C.5 The ASSET OWNER MUST disclose or otherwise indicate the reporting currency.

26.C.6 The ASSET OWNER MUST disclose the GIPS Advertising Guidelines compliance statement:

> "[Insert name of ASSET OWNER] claims compliance with the Global Investment Performance Standards (GIPS®)."

26.C.7 The ASSET OWNER MUST disclose the following: "GIPS® is a registered trademark of CFA Institute. CFA Institute does not endorse or promote this organization, nor does it warrant the accuracy or quality of the content contained herein."

26.C.8 The ASSET OWNER MUST disclose how to obtain a GIPS ASSET OWNER REPORT.

26.C.9 The ASSET OWNER MUST disclose if the GIPS ADVERTISEMENT conforms with laws or regulations that conflict with the REQUIREMENTS or RECOMMENDATIONS of the GIPS standards or the GIPS Advertising Guidelines, as well as the manner in which the laws or regulations conflict with the GIPS standards or the GIPS Advertising Guidelines.

 | **33**

26.D. GIPS Advertisements for a Total Fund or Composite That Include Performance—Recommendations

26.D.1   The ASSET OWNER SHOULD disclose the TOTAL FUND DESCRIPTION or COMPOSITE DESCRIPTION.

26.D.2   The ASSET OWNER SHOULD disclose how leverage, derivatives, and short positions have been used historically, if material.

26.D.3   The ASSET OWNER SHOULD disclose the BENCHMARK DESCRIPTION, which MUST include the key features of the BENCHMARK or the name of the BENCHMARK for a readily recognized index or other point of reference.

26.D.4   If the ASSET OWNER determines no appropriate BENCHMARK for the TOTAL FUND or COMPOSITE exists, the ASSET OWNER SHOULD disclose why no BENCHMARK is presented.

26.D.5   The ASSET OWNER SHOULD disclose the ASSET OWNER definition.

GLOSSARY

ACCRUAL ACCOUNTING

The recording of transactions as income is earned or expenses are incurred, rather than when income is received or expenses are paid (i.e., cash basis).

ADDITIONAL RISK MEASURES

Risk measures included in a GIPS ASSET OWNER REPORT beyond those REQUIRED to be presented.

ADMINISTRATIVE FEE

All fees other than TRANSACTION COSTS and the INVESTMENT MANAGEMENT FEE. ADMINISTRATIVE FEES may include CUSTODY FEES, accounting fees, auditing fees, consulting fees, legal fees, performance measurement fees, and other related fees.

ALL-IN FEE

A type of BUNDLED FEE that can include any combination of INVESTMENT MANAGEMENT FEES, TRANSACTION COSTS, CUSTODY FEES, and ADMINISTRATIVE FEES. ALL-IN FEES are typically offered in certain jurisdictions where asset management, brokerage, and custody services are offered by the same company.

ASSET OWNER

An entity that manages investments, directly and/or through the use of EXTERNAL MANAGERS, on behalf of participants, beneficiaries, or the organization itself. These entities include, but are not limited to, public and private pension funds, endowments, foundations, family offices, provident funds, insurers and reinsurers, sovereign wealth funds, and fiduciaries. ASSET OWNERS MUST have discretion over TOTAL ASSET OWNER ASSETS, either by managing assets directly or by having the discretion to hire and fire EXTERNAL MANAGERS.

BENCHMARK

A point of reference against which the COMPOSITE'S or TOTAL FUND'S returns or risk are compared.

BENCHMARK DESCRIPTION

General information regarding the investments, structure, and characteristics of the BENCHMARK. The description MUST include the key features of the BENCHMARK or the name of the BENCHMARK for a readily recognized index or other point of reference.

BUNDLED FEE

A fee that combines multiple fees into one total or "bundled" fee. BUNDLED FEES can include any combination of INVESTMENT MANAGEMENT FEES, TRANSACTION COSTS, CUSTODY FEES, and/or ADMINISTRATIVE FEES. Two examples of BUNDLED FEES are WRAP FEES and ALL-IN FEES.

(continued)

CAPITAL EMPLOYED

The denominator of the COMPONENT RETURN calculation, defined as the "weighted-average equity" (weighted-average capital) during the measurement period. CAPITAL EMPLOYED does not include any INCOME RETURN or CAPITAL RETURN earned during the measurement period. Beginning capital is adjusted by weighting the EXTERNAL CASH FLOWS that occurred during the period.

CAPITAL RETURN

The change in value of the REAL ESTATE investments and cash and/or cash equivalent assets held throughout the measurement period, adjusted for all capital expenditures (subtracted) and net proceeds from sales (added). The CAPITAL RETURN is computed as a percentage of the CAPITAL EMPLOYED. Also known as "capital appreciation return" or "appreciation return."

CARRIED INTEREST

The profits that the GENERAL PARTNER is allocated from the profits on the investments made by the investment vehicle. Also known as "carry" or "promote."

COMMITTED CAPITAL

Pledges of capital to an investment vehicle by investors (LIMITED PARTNERS and the GENERAL PARTNER) or the ASSET OWNER. COMMITTED CAPITAL is typically drawn down over a period of time. Also known as "commitments."

COMPONENT RETURNS

The CAPITAL RETURNS and INCOME RETURNS of a REAL ESTATE COMPOSITE or a BENCHMARK.

COMPOSITE

An aggregation of one or more PORTFOLIOS or TOTAL FUNDS that are managed according to a similar investment mandate, objective, or strategy.

COMPOSITE CREATION DATE

The date when the ASSET OWNER first groups one or more PORTFOLIOS or TOTAL FUNDS to create a COMPOSITE. The COMPOSITE CREATION DATE is not necessarily the same as the COMPOSITE INCEPTION DATE.

COMPOSITE DEFINITION

Detailed criteria that determine the assignment of PORTFOLIOS to COMPOSITES. Criteria may include, but are not limited to, investment mandate, style or strategy, asset class, the use of derivatives, leverage and/or hedging, targeted risk metrics, investment constraints or restrictions, and/or PORTFOLIO type (e.g., SEGREGATED ACCOUNT or POOLED FUND).

COMPOSITE DESCRIPTION	General information regarding the investment mandate, objective, or strategy of the COMPOSITE. The COMPOSITE DESCRIPTION may be more abbreviated than the COMPOSITE DEFINITION but MUST include all key features of the COMPOSITE and MUST include enough information to allow the OVERSIGHT BODY to understand the key characteristics of the COMPOSITE's investment mandate, objective, or strategy, including:

- The material risks of the COMPOSITE's strategy.
- How leverage, derivatives, and short positions may be used, if they are a material part of the strategy.
- If ILLIQUID INVESTMENTS are a material part of the strategy.

COMPOSITE INCEPTION DATE	The initial date of the COMPOSITE's track record.
COMPOSITE TERMINATION DATE	The date that the last PORTFOLIO exits a COMPOSITE.
CUSTODY FEE	The fee payable to the custodian for the safekeeping of PORTFOLIO assets. CUSTODY FEES are considered to be ADMINISTRATIVE FEES and typically contain an asset-based portion and a transaction-based portion. The CUSTODY FEE may also include charges for additional services, including accounting, securities lending, and/or performance measurement. Custodial fees that are charged per transaction SHOULD be included in the CUSTODY FEE and not included as part of TRANSACTION COSTS.
DISTRIBUTION	Cash or stock distributed to LIMITED PARTNERS (or investors) from an investment vehicle. DISTRIBUTIONS are typically at the discretion of the GENERAL PARTNER. DISTRIBUTIONS include both recallable and non-recallable DISTRIBUTIONS.
DPI (REALIZATION MULTIPLE)	SINCE-INCEPTION DISTRIBUTIONS divided by SINCE-INCEPTION PAID-IN CAPITAL.
EX ANTE	Before the fact.
EX POST	After the fact.
EXTERNAL CASH FLOW	Capital (cash or investments) that enters or exits a PORTFOLIO. Dividend and interest income payments are not considered EXTERNAL CASH FLOWS.
EXTERNAL MANAGER	A third-party investment manager hired by an ASSET OWNER to manage some or all of the TOTAL ASSET OWNER ASSETS.

(continued)

 |

EXTERNAL VALUATION

An assessment of value performed by an independent third party.

FAIR VALUE

The amount at which an investment could be sold in an arm's-length transaction between willing parties in an orderly transaction. The valuation MUST be determined using the objective, observable, unadjusted quoted market price for an identical investment in an active market on the measurement date, if available. In the absence of an objective, observable, unadjusted quoted market price for an identical investment in an active market on the measurement date, the valuation MUST represent the ASSET OWNER's best estimate of the FAIR VALUE. FAIR VALUE MUST include any accrued income.

FULL GROSS-OF-FEES RETURN

The return on investments that reflects the deduction of only TRANSACTION COSTS.

GENERAL PARTNER

Typically, the manager of a LIMITED PARTNERSHIP in which the LIMITED PARTNERS are the other investors. The GENERAL PARTNER earns an INVESTMENT MANAGEMENT FEE that may include a percentage of the LIMITED PARTNERSHIP's profits. (See "CARRIED INTEREST.")

GIPS ADVERTISEMENT

An advertisement by a GIPS-compliant ASSET OWNER that adheres to the REQUIREMENTS of the GIPS Advertising Guidelines.

GIPS ASSET OWNER REPORT

An ASSET OWNER's presentation for a TOTAL FUND or COMPOSITE that contains all the information REQUIRED by the GIPS standards and may also include RECOMMENDED information or SUPPLEMENTAL INFORMATION.

GIPS COMPLIANCE NOTIFICATION FORM

The form REQUIRED to be filed with CFA Institute to notify CFA Institute that the ASSET OWNER claims compliance with the GIPS standards.

GROSS-OF-FEES

The return on investments reduced by TRANSACTION COSTS and all fees and expenses for externally managed POOLED FUNDS.

ILLIQUID INVESTMENTS

Investments that may be difficult to sell without a price reduction or that cannot be sold quickly because of a lack of market or ready/willing investors.

INCOME RETURN

The investment income earned on all investments (including cash and cash equivalents) during the measurement period, net of all non-recoverable expenditures, interest expense on debt, and property taxes. The INCOME RETURN is computed as a percentage of the CAPITAL EMPLOYED.

INVESTMENT MANAGEMENT COSTS	All costs for both internally and externally managed assets. In addition to costs for PORTFOLIO management, they may also involve overhead and other related costs and fees, including data valuation fees, investment research services, CUSTODY FEES, pro rata share of overhead (such as building and utilities), allocation of non-investment-department expenses (such as human resources, communications, and technology), and performance measurement and compliance services.
INVESTMENT MANAGEMENT FEE	The fee payable to EXTERNAL MANAGERS for externally managed assets. INVESTMENT MANAGEMENT FEES are typically asset based (percentage of assets), performance based (see "PERFORMANCE-BASED FEE"), or a combination of the two but may take different forms as well. INVESTMENT MANAGEMENT FEES also include CARRIED INTEREST.
INVESTMENT MULTIPLE (TVPI)	TOTAL VALUE divided by SINCE-INCEPTION PAID-IN CAPITAL.
LARGE CASH FLOW	The level at which the ASSET OWNER determines that an EXTERNAL CASH FLOW may distort the return if the PORTFOLIO or TOTAL FUND is not valued and a sub-period return is not calculated. The ASSET OWNER MUST define the amount in terms of the value of cash/asset flow or in terms of a percentage of the PORTFOLIO assets, COMPOSITE assets, or TOTAL FUND assets. The ASSET OWNER MUST also determine if a LARGE CASH FLOW is a single EXTERNAL CASH FLOW or an aggregate of a number of EXTERNAL CASH FLOWS within a stated period.
LIMITED PARTNER	An investor in a LIMITED PARTNERSHIP.
LIMITED PARTNERSHIP	The legal structure used by many PRIVATE MARKET INVESTMENT CLOSED-END POOLED FUNDS. LIMITED PARTNERSHIPS are usually FIXED LIFE investment vehicles. The GENERAL PARTNER manages the LIMITED PARTNERSHIP pursuant to the partnership agreement.
LINK	The method by which sub-period returns are geometrically combined to calculate the period return, or by which periodic returns are geometrically combined to calculate longer-period returns, using the following formula: $$\text{Period return} = [(1 + R_1) \times (1 + R_2) \ldots (1 + R_n)] - 1$$ where $R_1, R_2 \ldots R_n$ are the sub-period or periodic returns for sub-periods or periods 1 through n, respectively.
MARKET VALUE	The price at which investors can buy or sell an investment at a given time multiplied by the quantity held, plus any accrued income.

(continued)

MATERIAL ERROR	An error in a GIPS ASSET OWNER REPORT that MUST be corrected and disclosed in a corrected GIPS ASSET OWNER REPORT.
MONEY-WEIGHTED RETURN (MWR)	The return for a period that reflects the change in value and the timing and size of EXTERNAL CASH FLOWS.
MUST	A provision, task, or action that is mandatory or REQUIRED to be followed or performed. (See "REQUIRE/REQUIREMENT.")
MUST NOT	A task or action that is forbidden or prohibited.
NET-OF-EXTERNAL-COSTS-ONLY	The GROSS-OF-FEES return reduced by all costs for externally managed SEGREGATED ACCOUNTS.
NET-OF-FEES	The return that reflects the deduction of TRANSACTION COSTS, all fees and expenses for externally managed POOLED FUNDS, INVESTMENT MANAGEMENT FEES for externally managed SEGREGATED ACCOUNTS, and INVESTMENT MANAGEMENT COSTS.
OVERSIGHT BODY	Those who have direct oversight responsibility for TOTAL FUND assets and TOTAL ASSET OWNER ASSETS.
PAID-IN CAPITAL	Capital flows to an EXTERNAL MANAGER or externally managed POOLED FUND.
PERFORMANCE-BASED FEE	A type of INVESTMENT MANAGEMENT FEE that is typically based on the PORTFOLIO's performance on an absolute basis or relative to a BENCHMARK or other reference point.
PERFORMANCE EXAMINATION	A process by which an independent verifier conducts testing of a specific COMPOSITE or TOTAL FUND, in accordance with the REQUIRED PERFORMANCE EXAMINATION procedures of the GIPS standards.
PERFORMANCE EXAMINATION REPORT	A report issued by an independent verifier after a PERFORMANCE EXAMINATION has been performed.
PERFORMANCE-RELATED INFORMATION	Includes: • Information expressed in terms of investment return and risk. • Other information and input data that directly relate to the calculation of investment return and risk (e.g., PORTFOLIO holdings), as well as information derived from investment return and risk input data (e.g., performance contribution or attribution).
PERIODICITY	The length of the period over which a variable is measured (e.g., a variable measured at a monthly PERIODICITY consists of observations for each month).

PIC MULTIPLE	SINCE-INCEPTION PAID-IN CAPITAL divided by cumulative COMMITTED CAPITAL.
POOLED FUND	A fund whose ownership interests may be held by more than one investor.
PORTFOLIO	An account representing one of the strategies in or components of the ASSET OWNER'S TOTAL FUND, including assets managed by EXTERNAL MANAGERS for which the ASSET OWNER has discretion over the selection of the EXTERNAL MANAGER.
PORTFOLIO-WEIGHTED CUSTOM BENCHMARK	A BENCHMARK created using the BENCHMARKS of the individual PORTFOLIOS or TOTAL FUNDS in the COMPOSITE.
PRIVATE EQUITY	Investment strategies include, but are not limited to, venture capital, leveraged buyouts, consolidations, mezzanine and distressed debt investments, and a variety of hybrids, such as venture leasing and venture factoring.
PRIVATE MARKET INVESTMENTS	Includes real assets (e.g., REAL ESTATE and infrastructure), PRIVATE EQUITY, and similar investments that are illiquid, not publicly traded, and not traded on an exchange.
PUBLIC MARKET EQUIVALENT (PME)	The performance of a public market index expressed in terms of a MONEY-WEIGHTED RETURN (MWR), using the same cash flows and timing as those of the COMPOSITE or TOTAL FUND over the same period. A PME can be used as a BENCHMARK by comparing the MWR of a COMPOSITE or TOTAL FUND with the PME of a public market index.
REAL ESTATE	REAL ESTATE includes wholly owned or partially owned: <ul><li>Investments in land, including products grown from the land (e.g., timber or crops).</li><li>Buildings under development, completed buildings, and other structures or improvements.</li><li>Equity-oriented debt (e.g., participating mortgage loans).</li><li>Private interest in a property for which some portion of the return to the investor at the time of investment relates to the performance of the underlying REAL ESTATE.</li></ul>
REALIZATION MULTIPLE (DPI)	SINCE-INCEPTION DISTRIBUTIONS divided by SINCE-INCEPTION PAID-IN CAPITAL.

(continued)

RECOMMEND/ RECOMMENDATION	A suggested provision, task, or action that SHOULD be followed or performed. A RECOMMENDATION is considered to be best practice but is not a REQUIREMENT. (See "SHOULD.")
REQUIRE/REQUIREMENT	A provision, task, or action that MUST be followed or performed.
RESIDUAL VALUE	The remaining equity that LIMITED PARTNERS or investors have in an investment vehicle at the end of the performance reporting period.
RVPI (UNREALIZED MULTIPLE)	RESIDUAL VALUE divided by SINCE-INCEPTION PAID-IN CAPITAL.
SEGREGATED ACCOUNT	A PORTFOLIO managed by an EXTERNAL MANAGER.
SHOULD	A provision, task, or action that is RECOMMENDED to be followed or performed and is considered to be best practice but is not REQUIRED.
SHOULD NOT	A task or action that is RECOMMENDED not to be followed or performed and is considered best practice not to do so.
SIDE POCKET	A type of account used mainly in alternative investment POOLED FUNDS to separate ILLIQUID INVESTMENTS or distressed assets from other, more liquid investments or to segregate investments held for a special purpose from other investments. SIDE POCKETS are typically not available for investing for new POOLED FUND investors that invest after the SIDE POCKET was created.
SINCE-INCEPTION	For COMPOSITES, from the COMPOSITE INCEPTION DATE. For TOTAL FUNDS, from the TOTAL FUND INCEPTION DATE.
SUPPLEMENTAL INFORMATION	Any PERFORMANCE-RELATED INFORMATION included as part of a GIPS ASSET OWNER REPORT that supplements or enhances the REQUIREMENTS and/or RECOMMENDATIONS of the GIPS standards.
THEORETICAL PERFORMANCE	Performance that is not derived from a PORTFOLIO, COMPOSITE, or TOTAL FUND with actual assets invested in the strategy presented. THEORETICAL PERFORMANCE includes model, backtested, hypothetical, simulated, indicative, EX ANTE, and forward-looking performance.
TIME-WEIGHTED RETURN (TWR)	A method of calculating period-by-period returns that reflects the change in value and negates the effects of EXTERNAL CASH FLOWS.
TOTAL ASSET OWNER ASSETS	All discretionary and non-discretionary assets for which an ASSET OWNER has investment management responsibility. TOTAL ASSET OWNER ASSETS include assets assigned to an EXTERNAL MANAGER provided the ASSET OWNER has discretion over the selection of the EXTERNAL MANAGER.

TOTAL FUND	A pool of assets managed by an ASSET OWNER according to a specific investment mandate, which is typically composed of multiple asset classes. The TOTAL FUND usually consists of underlying PORTFOLIOS, each representing one of the strategies used to achieve the ASSET OWNER's investment mandate.
TOTAL FUND DESCRIPTION	General information regarding the TOTAL FUND's investment mandate, objective, or strategy, and is expected to include the following:

- The TOTAL FUND's asset allocation as of the most recent annual period end.
- The TOTAL FUND's investment objective.
- The TOTAL FUND's material risks.
- The actuarial rate of return or spending policy description.
- A description of the asset classes and/or other groupings within the TOTAL FUND, such as the composition of the asset class, strategy used, types of management used (e.g., active, passive, internal, external), and relevant exposures.
- How leverage, derivatives, and short positions may be used, if they are a material part of the strategy.
- If ILLIQUID INVESTMENTS are a material part of the strategy.

TOTAL FUND INCEPTION DATE	The date when the TOTAL FUND's performance track record begins.
TOTAL FUND TERMINATION DATE	The date when the TOTAL FUND's track record ends.
TOTAL RETURN	The rate of return that includes the realized and unrealized gains and losses plus income for the measurement period.
TOTAL VALUE	RESIDUAL VALUE plus DISTRIBUTIONS.
TRADE DATE ACCOUNTING	Recognizing the asset or liability on the date of the purchase or sale and not on the settlement date. Recognizing the asset or liability within three business days of the date upon which the transaction is entered (trade date, T + 1, T + 2, or T + 3) satisfies the TRADE DATE ACCOUNTING REQUIREMENT for purposes of the GIPS standards.

(continued)

TRANSACTION COSTS	The costs of buying or selling investments. These costs typically take the form of brokerage commissions, exchange fees and/or taxes, and/or bid–offer spreads from either internal or external brokers. Custodial fees charged per transaction SHOULD be considered CUSTODY FEES and not TRANSACTION COSTS. For REAL ESTATE, PRIVATE EQUITY, and other PRIVATE MARKET INVESTMENTS, TRANSACTION COSTS include all legal, financial, advisory, and investment banking fees related to buying, selling, restructuring, and/or recapitalizing investments but do not include dead deal costs.
TVPI (INVESTMENT MULTIPLE)	TOTAL VALUE divided by SINCE-INCEPTION PAID-IN CAPITAL.
UNREALIZED MULTIPLE (RVPI)	RESIDUAL VALUE divided by SINCE-INCEPTION PAID-IN CAPITAL.
VERIFICATION	A process by which an independent verifier conducts testing of an ASSET OWNER on an ASSET OWNER–wide basis, in accordance with the REQUIRED VERIFICATION procedures of the GIPS standards.
VERIFICATION REPORT	A report issued by an independent verifier after a VERIFICATION has been performed.

APPENDIX A: SAMPLE TOTAL FUND GIPS ASSET OWNER REPORTS

SAMPLE 1   TOTAL FUND WITH TIME-WEIGHTED RETURNS

Genius University Endowment
Total Fund
1 January 2020 to 31 December 2020

				3-Year Annualized Standard Deviation			As of 31 December	
Year	Total Fund Gross Return (%)	Total Fund Net Return (%)	Blended Benchmark Return (%)	Total Fund (Net) (%)	Blended Benchmark (%)	Number of Portfolios	Externally Managed Assets (%)	Total Fund Assets (Equals Total Asset Owner Assets) ($ M)
2020	2.53	2.48	2.99	n/a	n/a	15	100	155.4

1. Genius University Endowment (GUE) claims compliance with the Global Investment Performance Standards (GIPS®) and has prepared and presented this report in compliance with the GIPS standards. GUE has not been independently verified.

2. For the purpose of complying with the GIPS standards, the asset owner is defined as the Genius University Endowment, established in 1972 by the Genius University Investment Committee of the Genius Corporation and is the manager of the GUE's assets. The Total Fund was created and established in 1972. GUE has been in compliance with the GIPS standards since 1 January 2020.

3. The Total Fund includes all discretionary assets managed by GUE for the benefit of Genius University's endowment. The Total Fund has used external managers since February 2002. The assets of the Total Fund are equal to the assets of GUE.

4. The Total Fund blended benchmark is calculated monthly using a blend of the asset class benchmarks based on the Total Fund's strategic weights for the respective asset classes. Each asset class uses a total return benchmark. The benchmark strategic weights listed in the following table are as of 31 December 2020. Strategic weights and asset classes weights for prior periods are available upon request.

Asset Class	Description	Benchmark	Benchmark Strategic Weight 31 Dec 2020 (%)	Asset Class Weight 31 Dec 2020 (%)
Absolute Return	Absolute return investments are expected to generate high long-term real returns by exploiting market inefficiencies. The portfolio is invested in two broad categories: event-driven strategies and value-driven strategies. Event-driven strategies rely on a very specific corporate event, such as a merger, spinoff, or bankruptcy restructuring, to achieve a target price. Value-driven strategies involve hedged positions in assets or securities with prices that diverge from their underlying economic value. Derivatives are used in absolute return strategies.	Juniper 9- to 12-Month Treasury Index	23	17
Domestic Equity	This asset class includes active management strategies, aspiring to outperform the market index by a few percentage points annually, net of fees. Because superior stock selection provides the most consistent and reliable opportunity for generating attractive returns, GUE favors managers with exceptional bottom-up, fundamental research capabilities and managers searching for out-of-favor securities.	Desmond Total Stock Index	20	4
Fixed Income	GUE uses a passive index strategy for the fixed-income portfolio. GUE favors shorter-term government bonds and does not invest in market-timing strategies or credit risk.	Juniper 1- to 3-Year Treasury Index	9	5
International Equity	GUE emphasizes active management designed to uncover attractive opportunities and exploit market inefficiencies. GUE hires managers with strong fundamental research capabilities. Capital allocation to individual managers takes into consideration the country allocation of the international equity portfolio, GUE's degree of confidence in a manager, and the appropriate size for a particular strategy. GUE attempts to hire managers adept at exploiting mispricing in countries, sectors, and styles by allocating capital to the most compelling opportunities.	Smith All Country World Index ex US	22	11

Asset Class	Description	Benchmark	Benchmark Strategic Weight 31 Dec 2020 (%)	Asset Class Weight 31 Dec 2020 (%)
Natural Resources	GUE invests in equity investments in natural resources—oil and gas, timberland, and metals and mining. These investments share common characteristics: protection against unanticipated global inflation, high and visible current cash flow, and opportunities to exploit inefficiencies.	Jackson Associates Natural Resources	8	8
Private Equity	Private equity offers long-term risk-adjusted returns, stemming from the value-adding managers that exploit market inefficiencies. GUE's private equity portfolio includes investments in venture capital, distressed investments, and mezzanine capital. The private equity strategy emphasizes partnerships with firms that pursue a value-added approach to investing. Such firms work closely with portfolio companies to create fundamentally more valuable entities, relying only secondarily on financial engineering to generate returns. Investments are made considering the long-term relationship with the manager and are expected to be the first of several commitments toward the close alignment of the interests of general and limited partners.	Jackson Associates Private Equity	10	33
Real Estate	Investments in real estate provide meaningful diversification to the endowment. A steady flow of income with equity upside creates a natural hedge against unanticipated inflation without sacrificing expected return. Although real estate markets sometimes produce cyclical returns, pricing inefficiencies in the asset class and opportunities to add value allow superior managers to generate excess returns over long time horizons.	Farley US REIT Index	4	18
Cash	GUE invests in short-term investment fund portfolios to maintain a cash reserve to assist in university operations as needed.	Juniper 1- to 3-Month Treasury Index	4	4

5. Descriptions of the blended benchmark components are as follows. The Desmond Total Stock Index tracks the US broad equity market for companies of any market capitalization size. The Farley US REIT Index is composed of equity real estate investment trusts. The index is a free float–adjusted market capitalization weighted index. The Jackson Associates Natural Resources Index represents domestic securities that are classified as energy and materials sector stocks, excluding securities associated with the chemicals industry and the steel industry. The Jackson Associates Private Equity Index is composed of the top private equity funds that meet defined criteria such as liquidity, size, exposure, and activity requirements. The Juniper 1- to 3-Month Treasury Index includes all publicly issued US Treasury bills with a remaining maturity between one and three months. The Juniper 9- to 12-Month Treasury Index includes all publicly issued US Treasury bills with a remaining maturity between 9 and 12 months. The Juniper 1- to 3-Year Treasury Index measures the performance of US Treasury bonds maturing in one to three years. The Smith All Country World Index ex US provides a broad measure of stock performance throughout the world, excluding US-based companies. This market-capitalization-weighted index includes companies doing business in both developed and emerging markets.

6. GUE's spending policy, which allocates endowment earnings to operations, balances the competing objectives of providing a stable income flow to the operating budget and protecting the endowment's real value over time. The spending policy manages the trade-off between these two objectives by combining a long-term spending rate target with a smoothing rule, which adjusts spending gradually in any given year in response to changes in the endowment's value. The target spending rate approved by GUE currently stands at 5.25%. According to the smoothing rule, endowment spending in a given year sums to 80% of the previous year's spending and 20% of the targeted long-term spending rate applied to the fiscal year-end market value two years prior. The spending amount determined by the formula is adjusted for inflation and constrained so that the calculated rate is at least 4.5% and not more than 6.0%, of the endowment's inflation-adjusted market value two years prior. The smoothing rule and the endowment's diversified nature are designed to mitigate the effect of short-term market volatility on the flow of funds to support GUE's operations.

7. Investment risks are diversified over a broad range of market sectors, securities, and other investments. The investment strategy's intent is to reduce portfolio risk to adverse developments in a single sector or industry. The primary risks of the Total Fund are active management risk, asset allocation risk, counterparty risk, currency risk, derivatives risk, liquidity risk, and risks associated with fixed-income investing, including credit risk, interest rate risk, prepayment risk, extension risk, and valuation risk.

8. Returns are net of brokerage commissions, expenses related to trading, and applicable foreign withholding taxes on dividends, interest, and capital gains. All returns and asset values are calculated and reported in US dollars.

9. Total Fund performance is calculated monthly using time-weighted rates of return. Gross returns are net of actual external investment management fees for pooled funds. Net returns are net of actual investment management costs (internal and external). Investment management costs include internal investment department compensation, benefits, actual external manager fees, data valuation fees, consulting services, and the allocation of technology services and other overhead costs and expenses. Total investment management costs to arrive at the net return have averaged roughly 15 bps annually since 2000.

10. Policies for valuing investments, calculating performance, and preparing the GIPS asset owner report are available upon request.

11. The Total Fund includes all individual portfolios that are combined into one aggregate portfolio. As of 31 December 2020, 34% of Total Fund assets were valued using subjective unobservable inputs.

12. The three-year annualized ex post standard deviation measures the variability of the Total Fund and the benchmark for the 36-month period. The composite and benchmark three-year annualized ex post standard deviation and the three-year annualized returns are not required when the Total Fund does not yet have a three-year GIPS-compliant track record.

13. GIPS® is a registered trademark of CFA Institute. CFA Institute does not endorse or promote this organization, nor does it warrant the accuracy or quality of the content contained herein.

SAMPLE 2 TOTAL FUND WITH TIME-WEIGHTED RETURNS

Centerville Police and Fire Retirement System
Total Fund
1 January 2011 to 31 December 2020

Year	Total Fund Gross Return (%)	Total Fund Net Return (%)	Blended Benchmark Return (%)	Total Fund Assets and Total Asset Owner Assets ($ M)	3-Year Annualized Std Deviation	
					Total Fund (Gross) (%)	Benchmark (%)
2020	10.93	10.80	11.30	514.2	3.25	3.37
2019	12.73	12.61	13.03	461.4	5.03	5.32
2018	1.79	1.67	1.17	428.7	5.14	5.37
2017	14.63	14.50	14.86	412.2	5.14	5.32
2016	6.12	5.99	6.07	369.0	3.62	3.57
2015	28.26	28.11	27.99	327.6	2.88	2.84
2014	10.28	10.15	9.50	394.7	2.33	2.23
2013	17.78	17.65	17.87	368.8	2.88	2.81
2012	13.12	13.00	11.95	324.3	3.11	3.09
2011	12.84	12.71	11.60	291.8	3.10	3.09

Centerville Police and Fire Retirement System (CPFRS) claims compliance with the Global Investment Performance Standards (GIPS®) and has prepared and presented this report in compliance with the GIPS standards. CPFRS has been independently verified for the periods from 1 January 2006 to 31 December 2020.

An asset owner that claims compliance with the GIPS standards must establish policies and procedures for complying with all the applicable requirements of the GIPS standards. Verification provides assurance on whether the asset owner's policies and procedures related to total fund and composite maintenance, as well as the calculation, presentation, and distribution of performance, have been designed in compliance with the GIPS standards and have been implemented on an asset owner–wide basis. The Total Fund has had a performance examination for the periods from 1 January 2012 through 31 December 2020. The verification and performance examination reports are available upon request.

Accompanying Notes

1. For the purpose of complying with the GIPS standards, the asset owner is defined as the Centerville Police and Fire Retirement System (CPFRS), established in 1985 by the

municipality of Centerville as the asset manager for the Centerville Police and Fire Retirement System. The Total Fund was established in 1985.

2. The Total Fund includes all discretionary assets managed by CPFRS for the benefit of participants in the Centerville Police and Fire Retirement System. The Total Fund blended benchmark is calculated monthly using a blend of the asset class benchmarks based on the Total Fund's strategic weights for the respective asset classes. Each asset class uses a total return benchmark. The benchmark (strategic) weights listed in the following table were in effect from 1 January 2020 through 31 December 2020. The asset class weights listed are as of 31 December 2020. Benchmark strategic weights and asset class weights for prior periods are available upon request.

Asset Class	Description	Total Return Benchmark	Benchmark (Strategic) Weight (%)	Asset Class Weight at 31 Dec 2020 (%)
Liquidity Reserves	The liquidity reserves asset class is intended to obtain a high level of current income consistent with the preservation of principal and liquidity. Investments generally consist of US dollar–denominated short-term securities of corporations that are rated in the highest category (A1/P1 rating) by the rating organizations and in securities that are guaranteed by the US government or one of its related agencies. Credit quality is emphasized for preservation of principal and liquidity.	Juniper US Treasury Bill 3-Month Index	1.0	2.9
Fixed Income	The fixed-income asset class is generally fully invested in domestic and international fixed-income instruments and is composed of the following issuers: US government and related agencies; mortgage-backed and asset-backed issuers; foreign issuers; corporations, including investment-grade and high-yield; and emerging market debtors. The methodology used places an emphasis on fundamental economic, portfolio, and security analysis to manage sector weightings and maturity distributions. The fixed-income asset class seeks diversification by market sector, quality, and issuer. The asset class is primarily managed internally, with external managers used in specialist segments of the market. Derivatives, including swaps and forward currency contracts, may be used to	Juniper Universal Fixed Income Index, which represents the union of the US Aggregate Index, US Corporate High-Yield Index, Investment Grade 144A Index, Eurodollar Index, US Emerging Markets Index, and the non-ERISA (Employee Retirement Income Security Act)–eligible portion of the CMBS Index. The Juniper Universal Fixed Income Index covers USD-denominated, taxable bonds that are rated either investment grade or high yield.	20.0	18.4

Asset Class	Description	Total Return Benchmark	Benchmark (Strategic) Weight (%)	Asset Class Weight at 31 Dec 2020 (%)
	adjust the exposure to interest rates, individual securities, or to various market sectors in the fixed-income portfolio. Underlying exposure of derivatives for fixed-income investments may not exceed 5% of Total Fund assets.			
Domestic Equity	The domestic equity asset class includes domestic and international common stocks traded on US exchanges, American depositary receipts (ADRs), REIT shares, and domestic equity derivatives (including, but not limited to, futures, stock options, and index options). Sector tilts by style, economic sectors, or market capitalization are managed in accordance with the risk budget for domestic equities. A variety of portfolio management approaches, including quantitative and fundamental techniques, are used to diversify the source of excess return. Underlying exposure of equity derivatives may not exceed 15% of Total Fund assets.	Desmond Total Stock Index, which measures the performance of the largest US companies based on total market capitalization and represents approximately 98% of the investable US equity market.	35.0	34.4
International Equity	The international equity asset class is a diversified portfolio including both developed and emerging countries. Portfolios consist of international equities including international common stocks traded on US exchanges, ADRs and ordinaries, international depository receipts (IDRs), country funds, international equity derivatives (including, but not limited to, stock options and index options), and some debt instruments. The asset class emphasizes quantitative and fundamental management approaches and exposures to security selection and country allocation decisions. Managers have the ability to add value through currency management. Underlying exposure of derivatives for international equities may not exceed 8% of Total Fund assets. Derivatives include, but are not limited to, financial, currency, and stock index futures.	Smith All Country World Index Net ex US, a free float–adjusted market-capitalization index, denominated in US dollars, of approximately 49 countries. It measures the equity performance of non-US developed and emerging markets. The Smith All Country World Index assumes the maximum withholding tax rate applicable to institutional investors.	23.0	19.1

Asset Class	Description	Total Return Benchmark	Benchmark (Strategic) Weight (%)	Asset Class Weight at 31 Dec 2020 (%)
Real Estate	The real estate asset class includes direct investments and investments in real estate limited partnerships. Each real estate holding is limited to no more than 5% of the total real estate assets.	Calculated quarterly, the real estate benchmark blends two benchmark indexes. The benchmarks and their relative weights are as follows: Farley US Regional Property Index (FPI) (90%) and the Duncan US REIT Index (10%). The FPI is an unlevered total rate of return measure of investment performance of a very large pool of individual commercial real estate properties acquired in the private market for investment purposes only. The Duncan US REIT Index is a float-adjusted market-capitalization index representing approximately 75 companies and designed to measure US equity REIT performance.	12.0	12.8
Private Equity	Private equity investments primarily include venture and buyout/growth opportunities. Risk is diversified by investing across such different types of private equity as venture capital, leveraged buyouts, and international funds. Private equity risk is also diversified by investing across vintage years, industry sectors, investment size, development stage, and geography. CPFRS typically invests as a limited partner in closed-end partnerships. Because of the nature of private equity, substantially all investments in this asset class are valued using market-based inputs that are comparable but subjective in nature because of the lack of widely observable inputs.	The private equity benchmark is 1% above the domestic public equity market (Desmond Total Stock Index).	9.0	12.4

 |

3. The assets of CPFRS are managed in accordance with the risk budget for the Total Fund and the individual asset classes. The Total Fund's investment objective is to earn, over moving 25-year periods, an annualized return that equals or exceeds the actuarial rate of return, approved by the Centerville Police and Fire Retirement Board (Board), to value the liabilities of CPFRS. As of 31 December 2020, the actuarial rate of return is 7.5%. Since 2002, CPFRS has hired external managers to actively manage selected portfolios. The percentage of externally managed assets for the Total Fund was 39% as of 31 December 2020. The Total Fund's asset allocation is designed to provide high long-term return at optimal risk consistent with the Board's expected long-term objectives. Investment risks are diversified across a broad range of market sectors, securities, and other investments. This strategy reduces portfolio risk to adverse developments in sectors and issuers experiencing unusual difficulties. The primary risks of the Total Fund include asset allocation risk and liquidity risk.

4. Returns are net of brokerage commissions, expenses related to trading, and applicable foreign withholding taxes on dividends, interest, and capital gains. All returns and asset values are expressed in US dollars.

   Total Fund performance is calculated monthly using time-weighted rates of return and reflects the deduction of transaction costs. Gross returns are net of actual external investment management fees for pooled funds. Net returns are net of all investment management costs (internal and external). Investment management costs include internal investment department compensation, benefits, actual external manager fees, data valuation fees, investment research services, custodian fees, performance measurement services, and the allocation of technology services and other overhead costs and expenses, such as human resources. Total investment management costs to arrive at the net return have ranged from 11 bps to 13 bps per year over the past 10 years. All returns are gross of reclaimable withholding taxes on interest income and dividends.

   Policies for valuing investments, calculating performance, and preparing GIPS asset owner reports are available upon request.

5. The Total Fund includes all individual portfolios that are combined into one aggregate portfolio. The combined portfolio's performance reflects the plan's overall mandate.

6. The three-year annualized ex post standard deviation measures the variability of the composite and the benchmark for the 36-month period.

7. GIPS® is a registered trademark of CFA Institute. CFA Institute does not endorse or promote this organization, nor does it warrant the accuracy or quality of the content contained herein.

Supplemental Information

The information in the following table is supplemental to the Total Fund presented on the previous pages. Performance information is for the period 1 January 2020 through 31 December 2020.

Fund/Asset Class	Gross Return (%)	Benchmark Return (%)	Number of Portfolios	Assets ($ M)	% of Fund Assets	% of Externally Managed Assets
Total Fund	10.93	11.30	28	514.2	100.0	39.0
Liquidity Reserves	0.12	0.05	1	14.9	2.9	2.9
Fixed Income	−0.97	−1.35	4	94.6	18.4	5.3
Domestic Equity	16.94	17.55	3	176.9	34.4	22.0
International Equity	10.17	12.65	5	98.2	19.1	5.6
Real Estate	10.59	10.07	7	65.8	12.8	12.8
Private Equity	15.94	14.55	8	63.8	12.4	12.4

Total Fund and asset class benchmarks as of 31 December 2020 are as follows:

Fund/Asset Class	Benchmark
Total Fund	Total Fund blended benchmark
Liquidity Reserves	Juniper US Treasury Bill 3-Month Index
Fixed Income	Juniper Universal Fixed Income Index
Domestic Equity	Desmond Total Stock Index
International Equity	Smith All Country World Index Net ex US
Real Estate	Real Estate blended benchmark
Private Equity	1% above the Desmond Total Stock Index

Please refer to Note 2 earlier in the report for further discussion of the Total Fund and asset class benchmarks.

Returns are net of brokerage commissions, expenses related to trading, and applicable foreign withholding taxes on dividends, interest, and capital gains. All returns are expressed in US dollars. As of 31 December 2020, 16% of Total Fund assets were valued using subjective unobservable inputs.

Total Fund and asset class returns are calculated as follows:

The Total Fund is valued monthly and when cash flows exceed 10% of Total Fund assets. Total Fund performance is calculated monthly using the Modified Dietz method. The Total Fund gross return is net of transaction costs, actual external investment management fees for pooled funds, and actual management fees for externally managed real estate and alternative investments. The Total Fund return net of all investment management costs (internal and external) was 10.80% for the year ending 31 December 2020. The Total Fund underperformed its Total Fund benchmark by 0.50% net of all investment management costs over this same period. Costs are reported annually by XYZ Benchmarking Inc. on a calendar year basis. Investment management costs include internal investment department salaries, performance incentives, benefits, actual external manager fees, and the allocation of information technology services (ITS) costs and other overhead expenses.

Fixed-income performance is calculated monthly using the Modified Dietz method. Performance of the internally managed portfolio excludes cash returns because cash is swept daily into the liquidity reserves portfolio. Performance reflected above is presented gross of investment management fees.

Domestic equity performance is calculated daily. Performance of the internally managed portfolios excludes cash returns because cash is swept daily into the liquidity reserves portfolio. Performance reflected in this report is presented gross of investment management fees.

International equity performance is calculated daily. Performance of all portfolios in this asset class includes cash returns. Performance reflected in this report is presented gross of investment management fees.

Real estate performance is calculated monthly using the Modified Dietz method with valuation changes reported monthly. Internally managed direct real estate investments are valued by an external appraiser once every three years and by an internal valuation quarterly. Valuations of externally managed commingled real estate funds are determined by the underlying investment manager quarterly, with supporting financial statements when available. Real estate performance excludes cash returns because cash is swept daily into the liquidity reserves portfolio. Performance reflected in this report is presented gross of internal investment management costs and net of external investment management fees.

Private equity performance is calculated monthly using the Modified Dietz method. Private equity investments are valued by the underlying investment manager with supporting financial statements generally on a quarterly basis. Typically, there is a one-quarter lag in the values used by CPFRS, but the values are adjusted to reflect current capital activity. Private equity performance excludes cash returns because cash is swept daily into the liquidity reserves portfolio. Performance reflected in this report is presented gross of internal investment management costs and net of external investment management costs, including management fees, carry, and fund expenses.

Liquidity reserves performance is calculated monthly using the Modified Dietz method.

APPENDIX B: SAMPLE COMPOSITE GIPS ASSET OWNER REPORTS

SAMPLE 1 COMPOSITE WITH TIME-WEIGHTED RETURNS

University Retirement System Domestic Equity Composite 1 January 2018 to 31 December 2021								
Year	Composite Gross Return (%)	Benchmark Return (%)	Number of Portfolios	Externally Managed Assets (%)	Composite Assets ($ millions)	Total Asset Owner Assets ($ millions)	3 Yr Std Dev Composite (Gross) (%)	3 Yr Std Dev Benchmark (%)
2021	−1.59	−1.48	7	43	6,112	29,276	3.40	3.47
2020	7.88	8.31	8	46	6,412	29,878	3.47	3.52
2019	12.67	11.98	6	47	4,298	27,333	n/a	n/a
2018	3.95	4.00	4	50	3,233	24,984	n/a	n/a

University Retirement System (URS) claims compliance with the Global Investment Performance Standards (GIPS®) and has prepared and presented this report in compliance with the GIPS standards. URS has been independently verified for the periods from 1 January 2019 to 31 December 2021. The verification report is available upon request.

An asset owner that claims compliance with the GIPS standards must establish policies and procedures for complying with all the applicable requirements of the GIPS standards. Verification provides assurance on whether the asset owner's policies and procedures related to total fund and composite maintenance, as well as the calculation, presentation, and distribution of performance, have been designed in compliance with the GIPS standards and have been implemented on an asset owner–wide basis. Verification does not provide assurance on the accuracy of any specific performance report.

URS was established in 2002 by the University Investment Committee to manage URS's assets.

The Domestic Equity Composite (Composite) includes all portfolios from the Total Fund that are invested in domestic and international common stocks traded on US exchanges, American depositary receipts (ADRs), REIT shares, and domestic equity derivatives. The Composite does not include the effect of cash or cash equivalents. The benchmark is the ABC US Equity Index, which measures the performance of the 4,000 largest US companies based on total market capitalization and represents approximately 99% of the investable US equity market. The Domestic Equity Composite was created in 2020. Domestic equity has been managed as an asset class within the Total Fund since 1 August 2002. Composite gross returns are calculated daily using time-weighted rates of return but do not include cash. Gross returns are net of actual external investment management fees for pooled funds. Returns are net of brokerage commissions, expenses related to trading, and foreign withholding taxes. All returns and asset values are reported in US dollars.

A list of composite descriptions and the Total Fund description are available upon request.

Policies for valuing investments, calculating performance, and preparing GIPS Asset Owner Reports are available upon request.

Effective 1 January 2019, John Smith, the chief investment officer, left the firm and was replaced by Susan Simpson.

GIPS® is a registered trademark of CFA Institute. CFA Institute does not endorse or promote this organization, nor does it warrant the accuracy or quality of the content contained herein.

SAMPLE 2 COMPOSITE WITH MONEY-WEIGHTED RETURNS

Kora's Foundation
Private Equity Composite
1 January 2017 to 31 December 2020

| 31 December* | Since-Inception Composite Net MWR (%) | Since-Inception Custom Benchmark MWR (%) | As of 31 December | | |
			Number of Portfolios	Composite Assets ($ M)	Total Asset Owner Assets ($ M)
2020	23.85	21.52	6	98	2,155
2019	9.06	12.35	4	55	2,033
2018	9.32	7.56	2	40	1,890
2017	20.06	18.69	1	24	1,842

*Returns are for the period from 1 January 2017 (inception date) through 31 December of the respective year.

31 December	Cumulative Committed Capital ($ M)	Since-Inception Paid in Capital ($ M)	Since-Inception Distributions ($ M)	Investment Multiple (TVPI)	Realization Multiple (DPI)	Unrealized Multiple (RVPI)	PIC Multiple (PIC)
2020	250	75	8	1.41	0.11	1.31	0.30
2019	250	48	2	1.19	0.04	1.15	0.19
2018	250	35	0	1.14	–	1.14	0.14
2017	250	20	0	1.20	–	1.20	0.08

1. Kora's Foundation claims compliance with the Global Investment Performance Standards (GIPS®) and has prepared and presented this report in compliance with the GIPS standards. Kora's Foundation has been independently verified for the periods 1 January 2010 to 1 January 2020. The verification reports are available upon request.

   An asset owner that claims compliance with the GIPS standards must establish policies and procedures for complying with all the applicable requirements of the GIPS standards. Verification provides assurance on whether the asset owner's policies and procedures related to total fund and composite maintenance, as well as the calculation, presentation, and distribution of performance, have been designed in compliance with the GIPS standards and have been implemented on an asset owner–wide basis. Verification does not provide assurance on the accuracy of any specific performance report.

2. Kora's Foundation was founded in 2005 to provide funding for local animal rescues.

3. The Private Equity Composite includes all domestic and international investments in leveraged buyout and venture capital funds. These funds tend to have long lock-up periods (seven years or longer). We make commitments to the funds in various amounts, and capital is called as investment opportunities become available. Unfunded commitments are typically called in the first half of the fund term. In some cases, funds may also recall previously distributed proceeds from investment sales. Recallable distributions are treated as distributions when received. If the distribution is recalled, it is reflected as additional paid-in capital. This will result in cumulative paid-in capital being higher than total committed capital. DPI, RVPI, and TVPI multiples will be lower, all else being equal, because the recalled distribution will result in the denominator being higher. In addition, the PIC ratio will be higher. The composite's inception date is 1 January 2017, which represents the first investment in private equity. The composite was created in April 2017.

4. The benchmark is calculated using a modified public market equivalent of the XYZ Global Equity Index + 2%. Capital calls are treated as cash flows to buy the index, and rather than treat distributions as cash flows to sell the index, we compute the weight of

the distribution and remove the same weight. This modification tackles the negative NAV limitation that can occur with the traditional Long–Nickels PME calculation. The XYZ Global Equity Index tracks the broad global equity market including large-cap, mid-cap, and small-cap stocks.

5. The Private Equity Composite has used external managers for all periods presented.

6. As of 31 December 2020, 100% of the composite assets were valued using subjective unobservable inputs. The private equity investment valuations are typically reflected on a three-month lag. Valuations represent the general partner's last partnership capital report adjusted for any capital calls or capital distributions.

7. The key risks to private equity include liquidity risk, capital/market risk, and funding risk. Liquidity risk is the risk that investments may not be liquidated when funds are needed. Capital/market risk is risk that the valuations may not be realized because of various factors including political events, interest rates, currency exchange rates, and the economic cycle, among others. Funding risk is the risk that contractual commitments may require we fund private equity commitments when better investment opportunities exist.

8. Composite money-weighted returns (MWR) are net of actual costs, including transaction costs and all underlying private equity fund expenses, including external management fees and carried interest. All performance is reported in Singapore Dollars.

9. Private Equity Composite performance is calculated using money-weighted rates of returns. Effective 1 January 2020, external cash flows are recorded daily. Prior to this date, they were recorded quarterly.

10. A list of the Total Fund and Composite descriptions is available upon request.

11. Policies for valuing investments, calculating performance, and preparing GIPS Asset Owner Reports is available upon request.

12. GIPS® is a registered trademark of CFA Institute. CFA Institute does not endorse or promote this organization, nor does it warrant the accuracy or quality of the content contained herein.

APPENDIX C: SAMPLE GIPS ADVERTISEMENT

SAMPLE 1 GIPS ADVERTISEMENT WITH TOTAL FUND AND ASSET CLASS PERFORMANCE

Happy State Pension System Investments
Total returns, net of external fees only, annualized on a fiscal-year basis, January 1–December 31

1-Year Returns (2020)[1]

Asset Category	HSPSI Net Return	Index Name	Index Return
Domestic Equity	15.35%	Quest Equity Index	15.06%
International Equity	14.91%	Bindy World Index (Net)	14.13%
Fixed Income	5.00%	Gator US Bond Index	4.63%
Real Estate[1]	15.49%	Real Estate Blended Benchmark	15.06%
Total Fund	**13.08**%	**Total Fund Blended Benchmark**[2]	**12.59**%

3-Year Returns (2018–2020)

Asset Category	HSPSI Net Return	Index Name	Index Return
Domestic Equity	0.85%	Quest Equity Index	0.80%
International Equity	2.02%	Bindy World Index (Net)	1.77%
Fixed Income	0.57%	Gator US Bond Index	0.49%
Real Estate	0.48%	Real Estate Blended Benchmark	0.59%
Total Fund	**1.56**%	**Total Fund Blended Benchmark**[2]	**1.44**%

5-Year Returns (2016–2020)

Asset Category	HSPSI Net Return	Index Name	Index Return
Domestic Equity	7.54%	Quest Equity Index	6.92%
International Equity	7.91%	Bindy World Index (Net)	7.29%
Fixed Income	1.62%	Gator US Bond Index	1.53%
Real Estate	3.79%	Real Estate Blended Benchmark	3.54%
Total Fund	**5.82**%	**Total Fund Blended Benchmark**[2]	**5.37**%

HSPSI Long-Term Policy Objective[3] (10 Years)

Total Fund	**7.1**%

Happy State Pension System Investments claims compliance with the Global Investment Performance Standards (GIPS®). GIPS® is a registered trademark of CFA Institute. CFA Institute does not endorse or promote this organization, nor does it warrant the accuracy or quality of the content contained herein.

Happy State Pension System Investments (HSPSI) is an agency within the Happy State executive branch that manages pension and health benefits for Happy State public employees, retirees, and their families. HSPSI is defined and created under the Happy State Code, Chapter 201.00.

HSPSI Total Fund returns reflect all assets of the Fund, including both internally and externally managed accounts. Asset allocation of the Total Fund as of 12/31/2020 is domestic equity 42.1%, international equity 20.5%, fixed income 28.3%, and real estate 9.1%. The investment objective for the Total Fund is to earn, over moving 30-year periods, an annualized return that equals or exceeds the actuarial rate of return, approved by the Happy State Pension System Board, used to value HSPSI liabilities. As of December 31, 2020, the actuarial rate of return was 7.65%. Effective January 1, 2021, the actuarial rate of return is 7.35%.

As part of the Total Fund strategy, the following asset classes may use derivatives and/or leverage to gain exposure to certain sectors of the market:

- Domestic Equity: Exposure to derivatives may not exceed 10% of Total Fund assets.

- International Equity: Exposure to derivatives may not exceed 5% of Total Fund assets.

- Fixed Income: Exposure to derivatives may not exceed 5% of Total Fund assets.

- Real Estate: Exposure to derivatives may not exceed 1% of Total Fund assets. Activities may include borrowing funds on a secured or unsecured basis with leverage limited to 40% of the internally managed direct real estate assets. As of December 31, 2020 and 2019, debt as a percentage of these assets was 15.6% and 17.3%, respectively.

All returns are calculated and presented in US dollars using a time-weighted rate of return. All returns are net of brokerage commissions, trading expenses, and foreign withholding taxes on dividends, interest, and capital gains. Returns as presented above are net of external investment management fees but gross of internal investment management fees.

The Total Fund blended benchmark is calculated and rebalanced monthly using a blend of the asset class benchmark returns weighted by the beginning market value of each respective asset class for the month. Information concerning the asset class benchmarks and the historical calculation is available upon request. The Quest Equity Index is a market capitalization–weighted equity index that provides exposure to the entire US stock market. The index tracks the performance of the 2,500 largest US-traded stocks, which represent about 97% of all US incorporated equity securities. The Bindy World Index (Net) is a market capitalization–weighted index designed to provide a broad measure of equity market performance throughout the world. The Bindy World Index is composed of stocks from both developed and emerging markets. The Gator US Bond Index is a broad-based flagship benchmark that measures the investment-grade, US dollar–denominated, fixed-rate taxable bond market. The index includes US Treasuries, government-related and corporate securities, mortgage-backed securities, asset-backed securities, and commercial mortgage-backed securities. The Real Estate Blended Benchmark is calculated quarterly using 85% Gator Property Index (GPI) and 15% Bindy Equity REITS Index. The GPI Index is a quarterly time series composite total rate of return measure of investment performance of a very large pool of individual commercial real estate properties acquired in the private market for investment purposes only. The Bindy All Equity REITs Index is a free float–adjusted, market capitalization–weighted index of US equity REITs. Constituents of the index include all tax-qualified REITs with more than 50% of total assets in qualifying real estate assets other than mortgages secured by real property.

To obtain the GIPS Asset Owner Report, please contact us at HSPSIperformance@HappyState.org.

[1]HSPSI has been verified for the fiscal years 2016–2020, and the one-year returns for the fiscal year ended December 31, 2020 have been examined by an independent verifier. The verification and examination reports are available upon request.

[2]The Total Fund Blended Benchmark is calculated and rebalanced monthly using a blend of asset class benchmarks based on the Total Fund's policy weights in effect during the respective period.

[3]The long-term policy objective is a projected annualized policy return based on return forecasts by asset class before any value added. The HSPS Board expects the net value added to be 0.40% per year.

APPENDIX D: SAMPLE LIST OF TOTAL FUND AND COMPOSITE DESCRIPTIONS

1. **Police Officers Total Fund**

   The Police Officers Total Fund includes all discretionary assets managed by Any State Retirement System for the benefit of police officer participants. The strategy reflects the actual asset allocation approved each year by the board, based on the funded status, risk budget, and actuarial rate of return studies. Performance is measured against a blended benchmark using asset class benchmarks based on the total fund's policy weights as established at the beginning of each fiscal year. The longer-term investment objective is to earn, over moving 20-year periods, an annualized rate of return that equals or exceeds the actuarial rate of return approved by Any State Retirement System. The Total Fund's asset allocation is designed to provide high long-term return at optimal risk consistent with the board's expected long-term objectives. Investment risks are diversified across a broad range of market sectors, securities, and other investments. This strategy reduces portfolio risk to adverse developments in sectors and issuers experiencing unusual difficulties. The primary risks of the Total Fund include asset allocation risk and liquidity risk.

2. **Firefighters Total Fund**

   The Firefighters Total Fund includes all discretionary assets managed by Any State Retirement System for the benefit of firefighter participants. The strategy reflects the actual asset allocation approved each year by the board, based on the funded status, risk budget, and actuarial rate of return studies. Performance is measured against a blended benchmark using asset class benchmarks based on the total fund's policy weights as established at the beginning of each fiscal year. The longer-term investment objective is to earn, over moving 20-year periods, an annualized rate of return that equals or exceeds the actuarial rate of return approved by Any State Retirement System. The Total Fund's asset allocation is designed to provide high long-term return at optimal risk consistent with the board's expected long-term objectives. Investment risks are diversified across a broad range of market sectors, securities, and other investments. This strategy reduces portfolio risk to adverse developments in sectors and issuers experiencing unusual difficulties. The primary risks of the Total Fund include asset allocation risk and liquidity risk.

3. **Domestic Equity Composite**

   The Domestic Equity Composite includes all domestic equity common stocks, exchange-traded funds (ETFs), American Depository Receipts (ADRs) traded on US exchanges, and REITs. The composite is not constrained by market cap. The strategy uses a combination of passive and active management strategies. Assets are invested using both internal and external managers. Key material risks include the risks that stock prices will decline and the composite will underperform its benchmark. Composite performance is benchmarked against the US All Cap Equity Index.

4. **2018 Vintage Year Private Equity Composite**

   The 2018 Vintage Year Private Equity Composite includes all private equity investments with an initial capital call from limited partners in 2018. The composite focuses on investments in venture and buyout/growth funds. The risks of investing in private equity are funding risk, liquidity risk, market risk, and capital risk. Risk is diversified by investing across different types of private equity such as venture capital, leveraged buyouts, and international funds.

Manufactured by Amazon.ca
Bolton, ON

34739860R00046